INDIANS, BLACKS,
AND MOROCHOS

STUDIES IN LATIN AMERICA

The Studies in Latin America series features short works published by the Institute for the Study of the Americas at the University of North Carolina at Chapel Hill. Print editions are distributed by UNC Press, and the UNC Chapel Hill Library hosts open access digital editions. The series promotes new scholarship on Latin America and the Caribbean focusing on the social sciences—principally anthropology, geography, history, political science, and sociology—and featuring diverse methodological approaches and perspectives on vital issues concerning Latin America and the Caribbean, past and present. For more information, visit http://studiesinlatinamerica.lib.unc.edu/.

INDIANS, BLACKS, AND MOROCHOS

*Trajectories, Intersectionalities,
and Class Frictions in a
Neighborhood of Buenos Aires*

Menara Guizardi and
Silvina Merenson

Translation by Wendy Gosselin,
Christine Ann Hills, and
Menara Guizardi

INSTITUTE FOR THE STUDY OF THE AMERICAS

AT THE UNIVERSITY OF NORTH CAROLINA AT CHAPEL HILL

This book was generously supported by funding from the Office of the Dean of the College of Arts and Sciences at the University of North Carolina at Chapel Hill.

Suggested citation: Guizardi, Menara, and Silvina Merenson. *Indians, Blacks, and Morochos: Trajectories, Intersectionalities, and Class Frictions in a Neighborhood of Buenos Aires*. Chapel Hill: Institute for the Study of the Americas at the University of North Carolina at Chapel Hill, 2021. DOI: https://doi.org/10.5149/9781469666457_Guizardi

Library of Congress Cataloging-in-Publication Data
Names: Guizardi, Menara, author, translator. | Merenson, Silvina, author. | Gosselin, Wendy, translator. | Hills, Christine Ann, translator.
Title: Indians, Blacks, and Morochos : trajectories, intersectionalities, and class frictions in a neighborhood of Buenos Aires / Menara Guizardi & Silvina Merenson ; translation by Wendy Gosselin, Christine Ann Hills, and Menara Guizardi.
Other titles: Studies in Latin America.
Description: [Chapel Hill, North Carolina] : Institute for the Study of the Americas at the University of North Carolina at Chapel Hill, 2021. | Series: Studies in Latin America | Includes bibliographical references.
Identifiers: LCCN 2021015304 | ISBN 9781469666440 (paperback ; alk. paper) | ISBN 9781469666457 (ebook)
Subjects: LCSH: Social classes—Argentina. | Social mobility—Argentina—Case studies. | Social stratification—Argentina—Case studies. | San Telmo (Buenos Aires, Argentina)—Social life and customs—21st century.
Classification: LCC HN270.Z9 S63144 2021 | DDC 305.50982—dc23
LC record available at https://lccn.loc.gov/2021015304

ISBN 978-1-4696-6644-0 (pbk: alk. paper)
ISBN 978-1-4696-6645-7 (ebook)

Published by the Institute for the Study of the Americas at the University of North Carolina at Chapel Hill

Distributed by the University of North Carolina Press
www.uncpress.org

"I just want everything to go well and for people to have something to eat. I am working class."
Ramiro (Buenos Aires, February 2020)

Contents

Figures

Abstract and Keywords

Abstract

This book addresses the relationships between stratification and social mobilities in Argentina today, using an ethnographic study on class relations in the San Telmo neighborhood (located in the country's capital, Buenos Aires). Relying on the extended case method, we narrate Ramiro's life history. He is a worker who has lived in the neighborhood for forty years, striving to carve out his career through a network of micro- and macrosocial relationships that frame his daily conflicts. We start by synthesizing the debates on class internationally and in Argentina, establishing the study's initial theoretical frameworks, and describing the methodology used. We then reconstruct Ramiro's life, starting from his experiences in his home province of Tucumán and narrating his migration to and arrival in Buenos Aires, his settling in San Telmo, his labor insertion, and the class conflicts that he currently experiences. We conclude by presenting a tentative anthropological conceptualization of class.

KEYWORDS *Social Class, Conflict, Ethnography, Extended Case Method, San Telmo.*

Acknowledgments

Social research is a chain of events that entails the participation of various people. We rely on the support of these persons at different stages of each project, and this multiplies our gratitude toward them. Accordingly, we first thank the neighbors of San Telmo, the members of its social organizations, and the people who work there or who cross its streets daily. With kindness and camaraderie, they allowed us to accompany them and record their routines in our fieldwork diaries, interviews, and photographs. In this work, we focus particularly on the life history of one of them, Ramiro, whom we warmly thank as a representative of all the people who helped us.

Another special thank you goes to Alejandro Grimson, director of the research project that framed the study presented in this volume, who gave us the freedom to reinvent our objectives and believed in the potential of the adventures we proposed. We also give special thanks to Catalina Kranner and Martina Beldi, young anthropologists who assisted us in the fieldwork; to Edison Pérez, for revising the grammar and style of the text in Spanish, and to Christine Ann Hills and Wendy Gosselin, for their amazing work translating the manuscript into English.

Finally, we thank the National Agency for Scientific and Technological Promotion of Argentina, which financed our work through Project PICT 2017-1767: "Emerging Middle Classes in Argentina, Brazil and Uruguay: Self-Identification and New Horizons." Having public resources for research in the current Argentine context is a privilege. This research was carried out with an awareness of the social responsibility involved in using public resources at a time when they are both so necessary and so scarce.

Part 1. Conceptualizing Social Classes

Chapter One

Introduction. Anthropology *of* and *in* a Crisis

Our Initial Plans and Their Context

In the first half of 2017, Alejandro Grimson, an Argentine anthropologist, summoned a group of social scientists to a research adventure. At that time, we were going through a very peculiar period in the American Southern Cone. In the first three years of the twenty-first century, countries such as Brazil, Argentina, and Uruguay continued to strive to overcome the problems caused by the hyperinflationary periods that had devastated their national economies from the 1980s onward. The 1980s were deservedly dubbed South America's "lost decade" (ECLAC 2006, 91). But from 2003 onward, these countries began to show a favorable macroeconomic scenario, with the international market's revaluation of the primary products that these countries historically exported to the Global North. Returning to a concept used in political and media discourses since at least the 1970s, Maristela Svampa (2013) called this period the *commodities boom*. In the American Southern Cone, the current century's first decade was marked by the emergence of popular left and center-left governments buoyed by redistributive perspectives and a multilateralist vision of international relations (Arnold and Jalles 2014, 8–9)—the Partido dos Trabalhadores (Workers' Party, PT) in Brazil, the Kirchnerist version of Peronism in Argentina, and the Frente Amplio (Broad Front) in Uruguay. Economies grew and states generated cooperation agreements and treaties in different areas, sharing their consumer markets by importing and exporting to each other. In social terms, the political agendas were oriented toward legal reforms that were understood as progressive.

3

In addition, a significant change in social stratification was observed, with the emergence of what were called the *emerging popular sectors*: specific segments of the population that experienced progressive increases in their consumer purchasing power and access to various types of goods. These sectors crossed over the poverty line in the first decade of the new century, configuring themselves as an *emerging middle class*, according to different scholars. During Luis Ignacio Lula da Silva's PT presidential governments (2003–6 and 2007–10), forty million people joined the middle sectors in Brazil (Arnold and Jalles 2014; Kopper 2014). In 2012 in Uruguay, the middle classes (according to income) comprised eight out of ten households, accounting for 51.8 percent of the population, an increase from 45.5 percent in 2002 (Carvajal and Rovner 2014).

This expansion of the middle classes was a Latin American phenomenon and was not limited to the American Southern Cone. Moreover, it was not just a change in the material conditions of income and consumption: a simultaneous transformation occurred in social imaginaries about otherness and class boundaries. In 2010, most Latin American saw themselves as part of the middle and lower-middle classes, according to ECLAC (2012). The Latinobarómetro measurements carried out in eighteen countries in the region in 2012 observed that 26 percent placed themselves as "lower class," 31 percent "lower middle class" and 38 percent "middle class" (ECLAC 2012).

Although these transformations had a regional character, the massive adherence to the middle-class identity was particularly noticeable in the American Southern Cone. In Argentina, 54 percent of those surveyed considered themselves middle class, while 32 percent self-identified as lower middle class (ECLAC 2012). In Uruguay, these percentages were around 49 percent and 33 percent, and Brazil registered around 32 percent and 32 percent (ECLAC 2012).

Those grouped under the label "middle class" (both "lower middle" and "consolidated middle class") in these countries were heterogeneous. For example, in Argentina, 28 percent of the respondents self-identifying in these groups were independent or self-employed workers, 34 percent performed unpaid domestic work,

14 percent were salaried, and 24 percent indicated another employment status (ECLAC 2012). In Uruguay, these categories were around 30 percent, 38 percent, 14 percent, and 17 percent, respectively. And in Brazil, they registered 21 percent, 28 percent, 13 percent, and 38 percent. Thus, for these three countries, it would be impossible to adequately understand the economic dynamics of these new middle classes without taking into consideration multiple factors, among them popular identity perceptions.

However, from 2013 onward and even more clearly after 2015, the economic, social, and political conditions of the American Southern Cone began to change: prices for the primary products exported by the region's countries fell sharply on the international market, affecting their economies and states. These processes triggered a crisis that promoted a turn to the political right in the national governments, profoundly impacting the emerging popular sectors. These countries experienced setbacks in their capacities for economic, labor, and consumer insertion while suffering from the states' withdrawal of redistributive policies. In short, a new cycle of neoliberal policies was beginning in the American Southern Cone.

Part of the South American sociological and anthropological production on that time observed the centrality of *hate speech* in the daily experiences of the middle sectors. These investigations testified that this period of redistributive regression was characterized by the polarization of political scenarios and the proliferation of narratives endorsed by class-conflict rhetoric.

The concept of hate speech is portrayed as polysemic in these studies. It alludes to the various forms of public expression (discursive and/or performative) that promote attacking groups or subjects' human dignity, denying crimes against humanity (exterminations, genocides, state terrorism), or attacking minorities in "unlawful actions" (Díaz 2015, 75). Given this heterogeneity, these discourses "have few characteristics in common beyond being conditioned by heinous motives or, more precisely, by hatred toward a certain community" (Díaz 2015, 79; our translation). These studies also demonstrated that the positioning around these discursive developments constituted a political dilemma for democratic states (Díaz 2015).

Since 2016, these discourses have become a central node in interpreting social and political processes, particularly in Brazil (Casimiro 2018). There, the turn to the extreme right was supported by promoting an anti-PT hatred among the popular social sectors that contradictorily had been the biggest beneficiaries of his government's redistributive policies (Girelli 2018).

Hate speech has also become central in Argentina since 2008, especially after 2015, removing a series of imaginaries about the country's internal alterities. The period was distinguished by the political representation of growing polarization between the two heterogeneous blocs. The first bloc is characterized by anti-neoliberal and pro-human rights political positions (linked to popular sectors and generally associated with the various wings of Peronism and the Left). The second is associated with neoliberal and securitist political positions (related to sectors of the agrarian and financial elites and mainly linked to anti-Peronism and the right wing). This polarization created social wounds, dramatically cutting through family relationships, work experiences, collective life, and public spaces. It revived with striking forcefulness the racist, misogynistic, and classist structuring of the historical conflicts of otherness between Argentine sectors that are represented as opposing poles on the spectrum of social identities (Grimson 2019).

Argentine social imaginaries have assumed the configuration of a *grieta* (crack) since 2015. This expression is currently used to refer to the void that has opened up between the two supposed sides of this polarity, the popular sectors and the elites. The middle classes float between these poles: they are getting closer to the popular sectors in terms of their income or consumption, but they preserve a distinction expectative mirrored in the elites. The dichotomous imagination fostered by the *grieta* frequently eludes the fact that Argentine social groups are currently characterized by a social heterogeneity that is difficult to synthesize (Grimson 2015). In general terms, however, hatred seems to flow from one side to the other, making invisible both the internal diversities and the similarities across different Argentine sectors. This process was crucial for the election of Mauricio Macri, who served as Argentina's president between 2015 and 2019. His first campaign focused on a discourse about moralizing the state and regularizing the alleged abuses committed by the previous Peronist governments—particularly the Kirchnerists. Macri used to refer to this political past as a "heavy inheritance."

Grimson proposed that we study the emerging Southern Cone popular sectors' experiences at a time when their rise was showing clear signs of being threatened. Simultaneously, we wanted to understand the place of political polarization and hate speech in the recent experiences of these social groups. In short, our project sought to carry out an anthropology *of* these groups' economic and political crises.

We formulated the project with great enthusiasm and submitted it for evaluation by the National Agency for Scientific and Technological Promotion of Argentina. By the end of 2017, we were informed that our proposal—for a three-year transnational study of Argentina, Brazil, and Uruguay—had been approved and that we would have funding between 2018 and 2021. However, our plans were overtaken by the outcomes of the same crisis that we had proposed to study.

Reframing for Understanding

Becker (1998) reflected on social scientists' mania for excluding our stumbles when describing our research methodology and its processes. This omission, he affirms, leads to a curious alienation: it generates an image of research that omits its errors and the role of coincidences in the achievement of important findings. As a result, readers are left with the idea that researchers are professionals capable of controlling their entire experiment and experience, thereby removing much of the human, situational, and historical character from the research.

These reflections introduce the events that transformed not only our research plans but the entire Argentine social reality, forcing us to reposition our study and its objectives, goals, and plans. We had noticed a clear deterioration of Argentine salaries by the end of 2017, with currency devaluation; and exponential increase in the price of basic services such as electricity, water, and gas (which in some parts of the country were raised 4000 percent); and worrying inflation indexes, but we did not foresee the situation that would prevail after 2018.

Beginning in March 2018, the country has experienced a crisis characterized by the loss of financial liquidity (with massive capital flight), the substantial devaluation of the peso in relation to the dollar, and the start of an overwhelming debt process with international agencies—the most significant such crisis in the history of Argentina and the International Monetary Fund (IMF). In exchange for voluminous loans from the IMF, the Argentine government agreed to implement austerity measures that worsened access to public social protection throughout the country (for example, the closure of the Ministry of Health, budget cuts in education, and plummeting pensions).

These policies "attacked the sick, not the disease," as a common saying in several Latin American countries holds. In Macri's four years of government, the gross domestic product (GDP) fell by an average of 4.3 percent annually (Giarrizzo 2019). Macri assumed the country's presidency with an annual inflation rate of 30.5 percent and left office with the rate at almost 60 percent. Argentina's foreign debt grew by US$112.1 billion (almost 100 percent of its GDP), the largest in national history. Specialists have stated that this indebtedness could take a hundred years to be reversed. The dollar increased its value by 548.6 percent, with a severe deterioration in the national currency's purchasing power (Giarrizzo 2019). According to the National Institute of Statistics and Censuses of the Argentine Republic (2020a, 3), between the second half of 2017 and 2019, the poor in the country went from 25.7 percent to 35.5 percent of the population and the number of those classified as indigent rose from 4.8 percent to 8 percent. Thus, Argentina returned to the poverty rates it had reached in the previous crisis of 2001. At the end of 2019, 44 percent of the population was poor or indigent. A report published by the Observatory of Social Debt of the Argentine Catholic University (2020, 29–33) presents even more drastic numbers: as of December 2019, nearly half of all Argentines were classified as poor (40.8 percent) or indigent (8.9 percent). In this context, accelerated social changes meant that various aspects of our research proposal were no longer valid. The emerging popular sectors had dramatically lost the consumer purchasing power and income that they had consolidated in the previous period.

Between 2017 and 2019, Argentina's middle classes decreased by 14 percentage points (measured according to multidimensional criteria in addition to income), with broad sectors that had been assigned to this category falling back into poverty. This was the largest decline in the middle classes in Latin America in this period (ECLAC 2019, 29; Latinobarómetro 2018, 74). We could no longer consider studying what happened to the emerging sectors in their newfound status as members of the heterogeneous Argentine middle classes because they no longer qualified, and their problems and conflicts had suddenly become very different from those we had initially proposed to investigate.

Researchers are part of a society (or several); we are related to one state (or several). We live, suffer, and act in concrete political, social, and economic contexts. As Becker (1998) also posited, to assume that these contexts do not impact social research would be naive at best and ludicrous at worst. For this reason, it is essential to set out clearly what happened to us as a research team in this complex crisis context. With the scarcity of resources and the various problems derived from the substantive reduction in state agencies' personnel, research funds were cut or postponed (with great uncertainty about when they might be provided). We did not receive the resources to launch the first part of our project until the second half of 2019. With the exponential devaluation of the Argentine peso, the budget was greatly reduced, making it impossible to carry out the transnational ethnographic processes that we had proposed in Brazil and Uruguay, whose currencies had not devalued to the same extent.

But this was not all. The human, social, and political situation of our environment and our own lives became more intense and acute. Our salaries abruptly lost purchasing power, and we accompanied our students in the growing difficulties experienced by the public universities. We consequently reconfigured the project, changing the way we understood it. If we had proposed an anthropology *of* the crisis at the beginning, now we were facing an anthropology *in* the crisis.

To explain this shift, it is appropriate to define what we understand by *crisis*. Crises are social, economic, political, or symbolic processes that condition the instability (or rupture) of the frames of meaning (Goffman 2006, 23), questioning the referents within which the subjects signify the social processes. This definition also alludes to the concept of *social situation*, referring to unstable experiences in which the relationship between social limits and intersubjective action is disrupted (Gluckman 2006 [1961], 17). In other words, a liminal moment in which the social frames are not capable of ensuring the peaceful persistence of relationships (Evens 2006, 53).

Following Grimson's debates (2016), it is possible to differentiate these crisis situations into three "ideal types," to use Weber's (2006) terms. First-degree: in which an unthinkable and unpredictable event breaks out, but people process the new situation using the available social frames. Second-degree: in which the irruption affects the social frames themselves, implying a hermeneutical crisis, a shortage of interpretive tools. Third-degree: in which a transition time is opened up, rapidly eroding the general and consented worldviews (Grimson 2016, 150–51).

What Argentina experienced in the second half of 2019 was remarkably close to a second-degree crisis. We observed the deterioration of basic human conditions, the loss of shared explanatory social frameworks that allow groups and individuals to position themselves in this process, and the generalization of mixed feelings of hatred and political confrontation. All of these processes accelerated the reconfiguration of relations between classes and social groups, causing major disruption and simultaneously fostering processes of conflict in which people's economic, relational, and identity status was in dispute.

Considering these elements, we reorganized our analytical perspectives and oriented the project toward observing these processes. We decided to focus on class relations in spaces in the Buenos Aires Metropolitan Area, characterized by social heterogeneity. The crisis context prompted us to investigate the histori-cal character and the contextual dimension of the conflicts and identifications that marked the daily experiences of specific neigh-borhoods, seeking to understand how class position and situation intervene in the production of social borders and boundaries.

The Book and Its Journey

After the economic crisis that destabilized the Global North from 2008 onward, anglophone anthropology renewed its interest in the concept of social class. This led to new questions about how to intersect macrosocial analyzes—about the logic of the capital-ist mode of production in geopolitics—with the contextualization of social conflicts in their most local fashion, articulated with cul-tural patterns, forms of identification, and imagined community narratives (national or not) (Kalb 2015a, 2015b). Doing so meant assuming the criticisms (built from decolonial arguments and the Black and feminist movements) of the concept of class in Marx-ism and the perspectives attached to the notion of social stratifica-tion (originated by the Weberian debate). Doing so also involved an active dialogue with Global South anthropologies, which had cast a critical look at the uneven outcomes of turn-of-the-century capi-talism (Lins Ribeiro and Escobar 2009).

As Kalb (2015b, 15) suggests, the flexible accumulation and social fragmentation that characterize current capitalism imply the multi-plication of possible class positions. Therefore, people move and occupy situationally different identifications (overlapping contra-dictory and strategic uses). This definition of class as a conflictive and situational process demands (1) the assumption of a contextual anthropological approach; (2) the historicization of the interpreta-tion of social relations; and (3) the extension of the ethnographic gaze, correlating everyday experience with macrosocial, macropo-litical, and macroeconomic factors (Kalb 2015a).

Thinking about these critical inferences led us to dedicate our efforts to rethink the possibilities of the concept of social class theo-retically and ethnographically. The two authors of this book grew up in contexts marked by the military dictatorships of the American

Southern Cone and by the international geopolitics of the Cold War. The notion of class is part of the social, political, and academic semantics that crossed our lives and training but that has suffered significant ostracism since the end of the twentieth century. Banished from many academic discourses, the term is less and less known by new generations of social science students worldwide (Kalb 2015a). From our perspective, this selective rejection of thinking in terms of class limits approaches and dehistoricizes explanations.

Our effort to think about the limits, possibilities, and applications of the class concept in current Argentine contexts has resulted in this book. In the first part of the volume, we review the social science debates on class, Argentina's historical cycles, the country's political constructions regarding the middle and working classes, and the popular sectors. In the second part, we apply these reflections in an ethnographic case study carried out in a Buenos Aires neighborhood, observing the class configurations and relations in a context of crisis and conflict.

The ethnographic scenario of our case study was San Telmo, a fifteen-minute walk from downtown Buenos Aires, near the Casa Rosada, the seat of national executive power and various its ministries. The neighborhood is a transition to the southern corridor of Buenos Aires, an area of medium-low economic stratification with various impoverished sectors. It is also a tourist enclave with considerable colonial architectural heritage (which gives it a particular aesthetic). This neighborhood was selected because of the heterogeneity of its inhabitants and places and its configuration as an urban zone of transition, placed between central and peripheral spaces of the Argentine capital.

The search to extend ethnography by incorporating a historical perspective on class relations in the neighborhood (paying attention to both micro- and macrosocial factors) was a considerable challenge. We responded to that by adhering to the Extended Case Method (ECM) (Burawoy 1998; Gluckman 2006 [1961]). The fieldwork was carried out between the middle of 2019 and March 2020 with the participation of Martina Balbi, an anthropology student, and our research assistant. We explored the method's possibilities, tracing different strategies for treating the qualitative material collected. One of the exercises carried out to extend our ethnographic gaze was particularly pertinent: the use of life-history interviews with neighborhood workers to observe how multiscale processes were transforming their positions and situations of class.

This book has an experimental methodological character. Part 2 focuses on a single life history, that of Ramiro, a concierge in a building in San Telmo who has lived in the neighborhood since the 1970s. Through his migratory routes across Argentina's territory and his dislocations in concrete social relations in San Telmo, Ramiro's self-ascription as "a working-class man" is intersectionally crossed by the racialized assignments of his identity. In different spaces, he situationally goes through external identifications that classify him as Indian, Black, and Morocho. This last word is polysemic in Argentina, generally referring to persons with brown skin and dark hair. Nevertheless, it is impossible to assign a precise phenotype to the expression since it encompasses situational classifications regarding racial and social distinctions. It can also accommodate symbolic resistance, express affection toward others, or be a self-affirming way of referring to oneself. Ramiro assumed and appropriated all three terms as expressions of his self-definition at various times in his life. Therefore, we could not investigate his class experience without considering these racialized social assignments.

Based on Bourdieu's (2011) debates, we conceive Ramiro's life history as a *trajectory*. We reclaim his narratives, linking them to the historical class processes that, despite embodying themselves in our protagonist, respond to social constructions and the experience of a particular subgroup. Consequently, Ramiro's narratives guide us through a selective historical reconstruction of Argentina's political and economic contexts, helping us highlight their specific configurations in San Telmo.

In addition, navigating Ramiro's life history will be oriented by a specific objective: to identify ethnographic milestones that contribute to the theoretical debate on social classes from an anthropological perspective. This is not the place to anticipate discussions that can only be understood in light of ethnographic descriptions. But the racial dimension of Ramiro's social experience inspired us to establish analytical linkages among the concepts of class, intersectionality, and friction—the categories in the title of this volume. Thus, this book follows a circular itinerary from theory to ethnography and back again.

In chapter 2, we discuss our theoretical starting points by synthesizing the meanings of *social class* in the Marxist and Weberian debates. We show the articulation of these models in Bourdieu, clearly setting out our initial theoretical frameworks. This debate is not intended to be exhaustive or cover the multiple possible uses of the category in the social sciences and anthropology (tasks that far exceed this work's limits). Our specific objective is to point out certain debates taken up in the ethnographic descriptions.

In chapter 3, we synthesize Argentine sociological, historical, and ethnographic approaches to social stratification. We focus on contributions that analyze social mobilities and class identifications, describing five social cycles that frame research on the topic in Argentina from the nineteenth century through Macri's 2015 assumption of power.

Chapter 4 describes the methodology of the case study and introduces San Telmo, providing some information that characterizes the neighborhood while illustrating its spaces and settings with ethnographic photographic records.

Chapter 5 delves into Ramiro's life history and describes it chronologically from his birth in the province of Tucumán through his migration to Buenos Aires, his settlement in San Telmo, his work experience, and his current class conflicts, all of which are related to key aspects of Argentina's history.

Finally, in chapter 6, we pick up the analytical milestones indicated in Ramiro's trajectory to propose an ethnographically situated conceptualization of class.

Chapter Two

The Uses of Class

Few concepts in the recent history of social sciences have had as controversial and politically implied a trajectory as that granted to social class (Kalb 2015a, 50-52). Central to the twentieth-century arguments between capitalism and communism (Kalb 2015b, 1), this term has taken on a polysemic character that is difficult to synthesize (Carrier 2015, 28). Encompassing the heterogeneity of the uses of the term *class* (as well as its historical configurations and social-political outcomes) are beyond the reach of one single text. For this reason, we offer a selective recovery of the concept's genealogy, seeking to specifically locate certain notions applied in Argentine debates and in our research.

A substantive part of the social science framework around class is linked to the elaborations of Marx and Weber (Carrier 2015, 28). Although these authors' proposals are considered a parting of ways, they share at least five common analytical assumptions. (1) They assume that human beings are social subjects. (2) Both consider that people transform their contexts. (3) They do so restricted by their historical circumstances (Carrier 2015, 29). (4) They agree that classes articulate divergent interests that often clash with those defended by the imagined national community (Aron 1981, 45). (5) They understand class as an articulating aspect of collective life that is inexplicable if isolated from other social components (Kalb 2015b, 2). But what marked the theoretical disputes in the social sciences were the differences between the two authors rather than their argumentative similarities.

Marx assumed that the production of the basic material conditions for human survival—food, shelter, clothing—made up the founding *structure* of societal organization (2008 [1867], 208). His definition of *class position* corresponded to the place people occupied in this process (Bourdieu 2002a, 122). By participating in productive activities, people were framed by a specific set of social relations and simultaneously positioned regarding the possession or capacity to control the "means of production" (natural resources, human labor, capital) (Carrier 2015, 29). This combination of relational, spatial, and material attributes that define the position of a social group in the cogs of a productive mode frames what Marx considers a class (Carrier 2015, 29).

In capitalism, the proletariat are those who have no access to control natural resources and capital and can only sell their own labor. The members of the bourgeoisie, in contrast, own the means of production. Between them, there is a structural contradiction that constitutes the main engine of history by bursting into conflict. The dispossessed classes—those who have nothing to lose—can trigger this conflict, which Marx (2008 [1867]) calls "class struggle."

The Marxist argument also establishes that the conditions for the existence of a social class are dialectically linked to the possibility of its permanence in time. The production of a class thus implies the reproduction of the factors or relations that condition its positioning. By taking on the dominant-sector world visions, the proletarians distance themselves from their own class consciousness and reproduce the exploitative system from which they suffer (Lukács 1970 [1923], 76). Consequently, the concepts of social class, work, and reproduction constitute linking categories in the interpretative Marxist framework (Kalb 2015a, 54). Additionally, the idea of class unfolds a series of compound categories: class position, class struggle, class consciousness.

However, despite his frequent use of the word *class*, Marx never came up with a fully explicit definition for the term in his work. Seeking to solve these analytical complexities, his successors multiplied the term's possible interpretations. In the twentieth century, authors such as Lukács (1970 [1923]), wanting to understand the representational aspects of the class experience—the *superstructure*, in Marxist terms—inquired how individuals and groups perceived their belonging to a social class (the "class in itself") and how they positioned this perception in relation to the other classes (the "class for itself") (Carrier 2015, 30).

In another approach, Gramsci inquired about the role of power disputes in the configuration of the class inequalities. Thus, he expanded the definition of the proletarian class to the concept of "popular sectors" (or popular class) and later to "subaltern groups," observing among them a wide variety of political subjectivities related to cultural, racial, and gender diversities and the core role of cultural constructions and the state in the reproduction of capitalist domination (Gramsci 1981 [1975], 181). This turn inspired the inclusion of racial, gender, and colonial conflicts in various authors' readings of the configurations of classes and popular sectors in the Global North and South (Kalb 2015b, 5).

In Latin America, the Gramscian reading since the 1970s allowed the oxygenation of Marxist thought, breaking it down into a diversity of applications and interpretations that allowed the role of the popular masses to be located in the different economic and political crises in various contexts. Portantiero (1977) recovered the legacies of this influence, referring to it as "the uses of Gramsci."

In the 1980s, García-Canclini (1984, 69) offered an anthropological critique that aimed to make visible a more hybrid reading of the Gramscian concept of subalternity, arguing not only on the uses but also on the "limits of Gramsci." To explain the relations between classes, "we must reformulate the opposition between the hegemonic and the subaltern, including other cultural interactions, especially the processes of consumption and the forms of communication and organization typical of the popular sectors" (García-Canclini 1984, 70; our translation). Thus, contrary to what happened in hegemonic anglophone anthropology, the Latin American perspectives that redimensioned the impact of globalization in the 1990s (with the undeniable influence of García-Canclini) did so from a reading of cultural relations supported by critical reinterpretations of Marxism. In this sense, the theorization of cultural hybridizations in Latin America has positions that escape the apolitical provincialism ("the primitivist instinct") that Kalb (2015a, 51–52) attributes to the anglophone anthropology of this period.[1]

This questioning fed the anthropological reading of the centrality of racial exploitation and ethnic hierarchies established by colonialism (García-Canclini 1984). It also marked the explanation of the place of native groups in the configuration of social inequalities (Quijano 2000), establishing the impossibility of understanding social classes in the Latin American nation-states if they are abstracted from their ethnic and racial markers or historical processes of alterity (Segato 1999).

In another direction, the feminist approach proposed by Beauvoir (2018 [1949]) also reshaped Marxist reflections on social reproduction, making the centrality of female exploitation visible and assuming that the "sexual contract" came before the "social contract" (Pateman 1988). These readings acknowledged female subalternity as a key structure of posterior hierarchical forms of division and domination (ethnicity, status, class) (Segato 2010, 14–15). They argued that the female overload associated with family reproduction processes (emphasizing the unequal burden taken on by women in care work) and male violence were long-term structures in the subalternity of human societies (Segato 2010). Similar readings were developed by feminist women from the periphery of the capitalist world economy, fusing these questions about social reproduction with the Gramscian perspective on the autonomy of subaltern groups (Spivak 1988). This study agenda caused a redimensioning of the relationships among social reproduction, gender, and the role of the family in the social organization of class conflicts.

Weber's Critique

Weber focused his analysis on a radically different axis from that of Marx, believing that the differentiation of subjects' social locations resulted not from their place in the productive process but rather from their ability to access forms of consumption and negotiation (including the workforce) in the market (Carrier 2015, 30). In Weber's argument, class differences were conditioned by the possibilities of various groups imposing their interests and needs on the logic of operation and circulation of wealth. These possibilities would configure a specific logic of power, implying the ability of these groups (or people) to steer social relations in the direction of their interests (Carrier 2015, 31). So, relations would exist among the acquisition of wealth, the political control of distribution, and the willingness of the class. The Weberian expression *class situation* is used in contrast to the Marxist term *class position* to indicate the place subjects occupy in relation to access to unequal distribution of goods and services (Bourdieu 2002a, 122).

Weber (1978 [1922]) criticizes the Marxist argument on consciousness, indicating that a sense of belonging between subjects of the same class does not necessarily drive a mutual recognition. He assumed that such recognition requires shared values, morals, and sentimental constructions that are more common within status groups but can be unusual across the class itself given its constitutive heterogeneity. Members of a class thus could even carry out the same productive work but be radically apart from each other in terms of world visions and the attribution of meaning to social practices. Therefore, "classes are not 'communities' in the sense we have adopted, but merely possible (and frequent) bases of communal action" (Weber 1978 [1922], 43). Consequently, the term 'class' will be used when (i) a large number of persons have in common a specific causal factor influencing their chances in life, insofar as (ii) this factor has to do only with the possession of economic goods and the interests involved in earning a living, and furthermore (iii) in the conditions of the market in commodities or labor" (Weber 1978 [1922], 43). Moreover,

Every class may therefore give rise to some form of "class action," of one of the numerous possible kinds; but it need not do so. In any case, a class itself is not a community, and it is misleading to treat classes as conceptually equivalent to communities. . . . If classes are not themselves communities, then, class situations arise only in the context of a community. The collective action which leads to the emergence of a class situation, however, is not in its essence an action undertaken by members of the same class but one involving relations between members of different classes. (Weber 1978 [1922], 46–47)

This perspective inspired the emergence of the "social stratification" approach. This term alludes to organizing social subjects or groups based on indexes that quantify possession of goods and access to consumption (Duek and Inda 2009). The layers are ordered hierarchically according to an ascending pattern (often illustrated by a pyramid) that differentiates the subjects into the terms "upper, middle and lower class, or superior, medium or inferior" (Duek and Inda 2009, 38; our translation). This approach understands that "relationships between people lead to forms of unequal distribution of certain tangible and intangible goods, which have positively or negatively privileged classes as a result. These can be production goods, but also education and qualifications, goods that configure 'class situation' in the market and that correlate to 'opportunity structures'" (Rivas 2008, 374; our translation).

Latin American studies on social stratification in the twenty-first century have made visible the heterogeneity of identifications in the region's countries. Research by the Economic and Political Commission for Latin America (ECLAC 2019, 27) conducted in eighteen countries in 2019 shows that the region's middle class increased from 26.7 percent of the population in 2002 to 36.6 percent in 2008 and 41.1 percent in 2017 but fell to 36 percent in 2018.[2] Currently, "76.8 percent of the population is made up of groups belonging to lower or lower-middle strata" (ECLAC 2019, 28; our translation). Although the middle sectors grew until 2015, a general decline has subsequently occurred, with a trend toward impoverishment (ECLAC 2019, 29). Argentina saw the greatest reduction in the middle class during the period (Latinobarómetro 2018, 74).

But these numbers differ substantially when surveys inquire about class self-perception rather than asking individuals to specify their access to a multiple set of indicators. When directly questioned about their perceptions regarding identity and location in social stratification, 50 percent of Argentines in 2013 considered themselves "middle class"; in 2018, only 36 percent did so (58 percent of the interviewed considered themselves lower class and

4 percent higher class) (Latinobarómetro 2018, 75). Disaggregating the information on employment status and income levels of those who place themselves in the lower and middle groups, we find significant differences. For this reason, the literature developed in Argentina adopted an articulating approach, wagering on the integration of the "objective" and "subjective" factors of class identification. We place ourselves from this articulating approach, in dialogue with historical (Adamovsky 2009b) and anthropological (Visacovsky 2014) studies. These debates delved into the narratives of the classes, investigating identity uses in conflict contexts (Briones, Fava, and Rosan 2004), inquiring about economies and moralities, and observing transformations in values, ethics, and consumption (Noel 2020).

We carried out this articulation in part 2 of this book by picking up Bourdieu's proposals, which sought to connect Marxist, Weberian, and structuralist arguments. This gave rise to a theory that ties the Marxist idea of class "position" to the Weberian concept of class "situation," offering an interpretation of the inequality and differentiation processes that integrally compute "objectifiable," "symbolic," and "relational" aspects (Bourdieu 2002a, 123).

Bourdieu: The Articulationist Perspective

Bourdieu redefined the linkage between the relationships and the materialities of social groups, conceiving them as derived from possessing a set of capital forms (social, cultural symbolic, economic) that, distributed asymmetrically, constitute the "social field" (Bourdieu 2011). At the same time, he understood the social field as a sphere of collective life that was procedurally autonomous "through history around certain types of relations, interests, and resources" (Manzo 2010, 398; our translation). This autonomation process was forged by struggles and efforts tending contradictorily to transformation and conservation. They depended on subjects disputing spaces, putting their resources at stake in the "struggle to win" positions (Manzo 2010, 398; our translation).

Thus, subjects fight to appropriate capital according to the opportunities and limitations their social position conditions them to (in relation to the hierarchies and structures of distinction) (Bourdieu 2002b). In these processes, subjects simultaneously establish their location in the social field (the class in itself) and their distance in relation to others (the class for itself). These strategies are not neutral, even when a naturalizing discourse is used to justify them (Bourdieu 2002b, 67). They constitute an aesthetic sense (Bourdieu 2002b, 53) that involves incorporating narrative, practical, and performative frames. When these elements persist in time as mid- or long-term phenomena and are transmitted between subjects who share location and spatialities in the social field, they become "class conditioning" (Bourdieu 2002b, 99).[3] These are linked to the particular way the subjects bodily assume—as habitus—their cultural capitals.[4]

These investigations pushed him to formulate the concept of trajectory, with which he sought to sociologically define the limits and possibilities of the social movement of class groups and subgroups (Cachón 1989, 513) and theorize on the role of the subjects in these movements (A. Gutiérrez 2005, 24). Bourdieu pointed out that the trajectory of the subjects implies at least three dimensions of their possibilities for incorporating cultural capital: (1) that which comes from the history of their subgroup or class, very often given by their family unit; (2) the history of the social spaces or fields through which they pass; and (3) their own itineraries and personal stories through these areas (Cachón 1989).

These definitions imply taking into consideration personal trajectories as framed in family stories, traversed by large-scale political, economic, and social processes while at the same imbued with a local, daily, and microscale constitution. This led Bourdieu to believe that the family is one of the central spaces for the reproduction of social trajectories (Cachón 1989, 541), where the elements that allow the conservation of or rupture from the asymmetries of power (class among them) are disputed. Considering these debates, our approach emphasizes the trajectory and the role of kinship networks and productive/reproductive gender inequalities in the construction of class conditioning.

Chapter Three

Stratification, Mobility, and Class

Perspectives from Argentina

In this chapter, we synthesize the sociological, historical, and ethnographic approaches to Argentina's social mobilities and class identifications since the second half of the twentieth century. We focus especially on contributions that analyze the Metropolitan Area of Buenos Aires, collecting information on the social processes that frame our ethnography in San Telmo. We do not cover the vast existing literature but rather identify core arguments that will help us historicize the case study presented in the second part of the book.

Five social cycles frame research on class in Argentina from the nineteenth century until Mauricio Macri came to power in 2015: (1) the mass influx of European migrants (1860-1930); (2); the first Peronism (1943-55); (3) developmentalism (1958-72); (4) neoliberalization (1976-2002); and (5) the post-neoliberal period (2002-15). In each of them, we point out the limits and porosities between the uses of middle, working, and popular classes. We conclude by offering a synthesis of the factors that configure the possibilities and heterogeneities of social mobility in the country: access to education, gender, and migratory status.

The Migrant Influx (1860-1930)

The first studies on Argentina's social stratification go back to Gino Germani ([1955], 2010 [1963]), who analyzed the impact of the mass influx of European migrants, among other issues. Argentina ranked second worldwide as a destination for these migrants in the nineteenth and twentieth centuries, outnumbered only by the United States. The social ascent of these migrants took place rapidly, configuring what the sociologist calls "intragenerational mobility" (that is, people experienced it during their own lifetimes).[1]

In the first decades of the twentieth century, economic growth and occupational diversification pushed Argentina through a process of upward structural mobility: the middle strata grew, but a chronic shortage of workers occurred. Germani (2010 [1963]) observed the high rate of ascent from the popular classes to the middle-class strata, which accounted for 36.5 percent of the population of Buenos Aires, a percentage higher than that of São Paulo, Brazil (29.4 percent), and Melbourne, Australia (24.1 percent), for example. Until late in the twentieth century, the history and definitions of Argentina's popular classes almost entirely coincided with those of the labor movement—that is, with its struggles, the lives of its leaders, and the development of its unions (Roldán 2008, 200). Therefore, for many decades, the popular classes were understood as synonymous with the working classes (or better, as the institutionalized working classes). Gramsci's approach to the popular masses and classes (see chapter 2) started to spread only in the 1970s.[2]

Conversely, the period between 1900 and 1930, reviewed by social scientists from the 1960s onward, sheltered deep debates on the concept of the middle class. Different works accounted for the historicity, dynamism, and subjective processes associated with these Argentine sectors. Adamovsky (2013) pointed out the "residual" condition of the category in the research at that time: its boundaries were delimited by other classes whose objective parameters or criteria undoubtedly created more consensus—that is, those who controlled the economy (the upper class, the bourgeoisie) and those who sold their labor (the working class, the proletariat). Thus, to label oneself middle class implied "placing yourself (right) in the middle and claiming a spot on the map of 'civilization,' a symbolic operation with profound consequences" (Adamovsky 2013, 47; our translation). Among them, the historian Garguín (2013) pointed out the racial ones, particularly relevant in the histories of the origins of the middle class between 1920 and 1960 (see chapter 5).

According to Adamovsky (2009b), the category "middle class"

began to be used by the intelligentsia in the 1920s in an attempt to contain or erect an identity frontier regarding the popular classes' identifications with communism and anarchism. With the category's nuances, the Argentine Left—the Socialist Party and the Communist Party—showed signs of ambivalence and a certain difficulty in politically "positioning" the middle class. The Socialist Party may have managed to incorporate the middle class into its leadership discourse and policy of alliances, though not without suspicion (Adamovsky 2008).

The Unión Cívica Radical (Radical Civic Union, UCR) was founded at the end of the nineteenth century as cross-class party, that self-identified as linked to the people, the homeland, and the nation. Nevertheless, references to the middle classes were quite unusual and denigrating. The uses of the concept were outlined in the political discourse of the 1930s. But its definition was destined to update the classic liberal discourse: it was "counterinsurgent," striving to counteract the egalitarianism of the revolutionary movements. Thus, the UCR contributed to the discursive invention of the middle class but was not its founding political expression (Adamovsky 2009a).

According to Germani (2010 [1963]), in the first half of the twentieth century, almost 40 percent of the sons and daughters of skilled workers ascended to the middle class, mainly through three channels: their insertion in trade activities, technical-administrative employment, and skilled jobs. Half of the children of unskilled worker parents (many of rural origin) reached the skilled segment of the working class through factory employment or self-employment in trades (as artisans or workshop laborers) that enabled them to achieve an incipient economic accumulation. In Greater Buenos Aires, 40 percent of the middle strata and 20 percent of the middle-upper strata were made up by those of popular class origin.[3]

Starting in the 1930s, internal migrations (rural-urban) put the *población criolla* (population of mestizo descent) in contact with the population of European descent, causing changes: high rates of mobility from the popular class strata to the middle class and from occupations without trades to skilled workers. Intranational and

European migration had similar volumes in Argentina, although their effect on social mobility was remarkably different. People descended from mestizos and the popular class labored mainly as workers in conditions of greater exploitation.

The Justicialist Strategy (1943–1955)

During the first Peronism period, under Juan Domingo Perón, social mobilities were framed within the *justicialist strategy* (Torrado 2010). At that time, active income redistribution policies toward wage earners, direct public investment in industries and services, and subsidized loans for small and medium-sized entrepreneurs were promoted. This caused the "coexistence of upward and downward structural mobility flows" (Kessler 2016, 19).

Industrialization by import substitution opened up two channels of intra- and intergenerational mobility. First, the paid manual wage labor force expanded, thereby creating an industrial working class that brought together old and new workers. Never before had this class exhibited a "social density of such magnitude" or such centrality "in the dynamic core of the national economy" (Torre 2010, 193; our translation). Most internal migrants had been inserted in their towns of origin as unskilled or semiskilled (mostly rural) workers. Their transfer to the cities and their introduction in the manufacturing and construction industry as a salaried labor force (or as self-employed workers with a trade) meant intragenerational social mobility.

The massive adoption of the category of middle class in Argentina began precisely in this period (Adamovsky 2009a). At that time, being middle class was a way of differentiating oneself from the "workers." In contrast, the middle class was white, anti-Peronist, *porteña* (born in Buenos Aires), and Europeanizing (see part 2). However, going against the generally accepted idea that first Peronism was "workerist," Adamovsky (2009a) warns that Perón initially conceived the country as a tripartite organized community—workers/popular class, middle class, and oligarchy. This idea was later abandoned in pursuit of a binary division between the people and the oligarchy.

Developmentalism (1958–1972)

In 1955, the self-styled Revolución Liberadora [Liberating Revolution] culminated in a violent ban (lasting eighteen years) of Peronism and initiated a new political cycle (Grimson 2019).[4] The left's counterinsurgency discourse again placed workers at the center of development, while Peronism, having failed to mobilize the middle sectors, leaned toward contempt for them. In fact, the bloody Revolución Liberadora was read as a middle-class movement. The members of the intelligentsia soon realized their mistake, observing that these ideas fostered a ruthless criticism regarding the petty bourgeoisie, who had been incorporated into Peronism since the 1960s (Altamirano 1997). Given that the middle class had at times been part of Peronism's electoral base, their divorce was the topic of debate and controversy (Semán and Merenson 2007).

Some authors consider that in macroeconomic terms, the development strategy was markedly concentrating and excluding (Torrado 2010). In the early 1960s, the country was characterized by the weight and size of its middle class and by a consolidated working class with high levels of employment and good wages in South American terms as well as with broad access to social rights and a comparatively equitable distribution of income (Kessler 2016).

From another perspective, Dalle (2016, 97) analyzed the patterns of social mobility of people of popular-class origin in the Buenos Aires Metropolitan Area over the 1960s and 1970s. He noted the "occupational and educational opportunities that were opened or closed in the class structure, the limitations linked to the family's class origin and people's capacity to act on their circumstances" (Dalle 2016, 30; our translation). He concluded that in this period, short-range class displacements predominated, with ascending movements more frequent (24.9 percent) than descending ones (17.2 percent) (Dalle 2016). Upward long-range mobility (15.4 percent) was more frequent than downward long-range mobility (10.5 percent). Mobility thus constituted a descriptive indicator of the permeability of class boundaries beyond structural changes. But to what extent could this high level of structural mobility indicate growing opportunities for social progress?

The conceptualization and operationalization of the "working class" provide possible answers to this question. According to Dalle (2016), the concept refers to the identity formed by labor insertion that is mediated by a formal salary. This conceptualization was particularly coherent in Argentina in the mid-twentieth century, given the spread of salaried jobs in the urban environment, they had their most dynamic core though they were not limited to the manufacturing sector. The working class had improved its relative position substantially: the agroexport development models and industrialization by import substitution contributed to the configuration of an open and integrated social structure, which distinguished itself in the Latin American context between 1960 and 1970s. This phenomenon resulted from the opportunities for people of popular-class origin to advance socially, the breadth of the middle class, and the presence of a factory-based working class with a consolidated economic position and rights.

The research on the working class gave rise to the historical inquiry regarding the validity of Gramsci's notion of popular class in Argentina. With a brief interregnum, the period 1966–83 was peculiarly dark for historiography and social history. Among the young generations of historians, exile and institutional displacement were marked by contact with a Gramsci-inspired British Marxism that was concerned with the identities of social classes, their practices, and their values beyond their productive insertion (Roldán 2008, 211). These debates established a critique regarding the limitations and rigidities of the term *working class* that, toward the 1980s, installed the more ambiguous term *popular class* (*sectores populares*).[5]

Neoliberalization (1976–2002)

The *neoliberalizing strategy* was marked by the deindustrialization and concentration of income (Torrado 2010). In sharp contrast to the previous stages, an increase in "short-range upward intergenerational occupational mobility from middle-class positions in technical or administrative work" to "managerial and professional positions via the mobilization of educational credentials" was observed (Dalle 2016, 59; our translation). In addition, there was an "increase in occupational and educational inheritance in the higher-status segments of the middle class (professionals, managers, and capital owners)" and "a downward social mobility marked by the disappearance of salaried workers and employees in the public administration" (Dalle 2016, 59; our translation).

These patterns suggest a partial closure of the mobility regime that marked the preceding decades at the hands of increasing inequalities between the different class positions. Faced with exclusionary social processes, "popular-class families have fewer material and symbolic resources to achieve higher-prestige occupations. While the children of the middle class and petty bourgeoisie inherit capital or have the support of their parents to finance their educational career and the members of the professional or managerial middle class are in a better position to transmit their cultural capital, the working class usually only has labor or the specialized knowledge of a trade" (Dalle 2016, 71; our translation).

Two stages can be recognized in this period. The first, in the mid-1970s, marked the beginning of the transition toward a neoliberal model, with the concentration of the financial system, privatizations and external opening up of Argentine markets. The identification of the middle class persisted and was consolidated during the violent dictatorship (1976–82). Carassai (2013) studied the political culture of the members of the middle class, their relationship with Peronism, and their perception of the gradual radicalization of different forms of violence: social, guerrilla, state, and symbolic. She observed the contradictory social experiences of the middle class as a silent and silenced majority in a context of growing mobilization and repression.

With the return of democracy (1983), the presidential government of Raúl Alfonsín (UCR) (1983–89) gave pride to those identifying as middle class, who claimed their place as guarantors of the restored democracy. However, at the end of the "Alfonsinist spring," "low circulation of the concept of the middle class and a withdrawal from its identity meanings and its classificatory capacity were perceived from a distance. This went hand in hand with the relative disuse of the notion of class in general. By then, the notion of *gente* [persons] replaced both the notions of people and middle class in public discourse, merging them" (Garguín 2013, our translation).

Toward the 1980s, in parallel with the return to democracy, historians carried out several studies of daily life in neighborhoods and their inhabitants' cultural consumption, religiosity, and political participation, multiplying the number of case studies thematizing the fragmentation of the social field. Anthropologists and sociologists also followed these trends, bringing their own innovations to this approach. The research carried out at the neighborhood level became one of the main ways to explore the future of the popular, thus starting "the definitive dismissal of the category of social class [for] writing an alternative history to both the traditional neighborhood historiographies and the Marxist ones" (Roldán 2008, 218; our translation). Therefore, historiography took a certain distance from structural studies linked to economic accumulation models (Torrado 2010) "strongly focused on the analysis of labor markets and poverty" (Benza et al. 2016, 182). This agenda that marked Argentine sociology also had its breakaways (Benza et al. 2016). Jelin and her collaborators' qualitative methodologies clearly had an innovative character (Jelin, Vila, and D'Amico 1987; Jelin 1993) derived from their approach, which was linked to the construction of citizenship and the research techniques they used (Benza et al. 2016, 187). In addition to making room for class self-ascriptions, these works noted the political ties of the popular class as a dimension of daily life.

If the notion of popular class became legitimized in some historiography and qualitative sociological studies, the same was not true when it came to addressing "the obsession to understand the Peronist phenomenon and explain the unshakable adhesion mechanisms of its social base (the working class)" (Roldán 2008, 203; our translation).

In writings such as those by Murmis and Portantiero (1971) and Torre (1989), *class* is an unavoidable cornerstone for discussing Germani's thesis, among other issues. First, this category explains the alliance between a populist elite and a labor movement that consolidates and gains institutional weight but loses its autonomy. Second, it shows us the configuration of a political identity capable of creating mass unionism that integrates and subordinates the workers to the interests of the ruling elite. These works make up the classical paradigm on the relations between the labor movement and the first Peronism.

The second stage of the *neoliberalizing strategy*, in the 1990s, marked the consolidation of the "neoliberal order" (Pucciarelli 2011) within the framework of Peronist Carlos Menem's two presidential terms (1989–99). His arrival in power was the subject of various explanatory gambles focused on constructing broad alliances, from traditional Peronism to sectors of the middle and upper classes historically identified with other parties (Obradovich 2016). This phenomenon allowed a consensus to develop on the need to introduce "structural reforms" justified through antistate rhetoric. Its broad, even antagonistic, electoral base was explained by the ability of "liberal Peronism" (Pucciarelli 2011) to respond to multiple sectoral interests (Beltrán 2011; Heredia 2011). It was also fostered by the new role assumed by the media and Menem's capacity to sustain a constant tension between rupture and continuity with the Peronist tradition (Canelo 2011).

Toward the end of the 1990s, the deindustrialization and unemployment of skilled workers reached their highest levels during the crisis of 1998–2002, signaling the final phase of the productive industrial disarticulation. This was accompanied by an antiunion policy that attacked organizations whose members defined themselves through shared notions such as the idea of the working class (see chapter 5).

Analyzing the crisis that put an end to Fernando de la Rua's government (1999–2001), Visacovsky investigated how it was experienced by those who identified as (or were seen to be) middle class in Buenos Aires. He registered "the changes in their levels and lifestyles, and how the meanings of these related to their identity" (Visacovsky 2008, 9; our translation). He concluded that "the color of the middle class is white, to the extent of being decisive when it comes to including or excluding individuals, neighborhoods, bodies, clothing, food and drink, music, sports, or television programs" (Visacovsky 2008, 16; our translation).

According to Adamovsky (2009a), this second neoliberal stage destroyed social ties; the middle class had served the neoliberal program, in the first years at least, but a many of its members had ended up impoverished. Their brief encounter with the popular classes crystallized in 2001. However, the public discourse featured "a classifying device that builds up middle-class neighbors mobilized spontaneously, peacefully, and autonomously to oppose those from the popular classes who acted as mere clients of a plundering and corrupt government" (Garguín 2013, 2; our translation).

The growth the Argentine middle class had witnessed since the beginning of the twentieth century—albeit at different velocities and varied conditions across the decades—was thus interrupted (Benza 2016, 117). In the 1990s, the country "experienced massive impoverishment" that evidenced the segmentation, heterogenization, and polarization of its society (Minujin and López 1994, 92). The increase in income inequality determined the "winners" and the "losers" of the neoliberal capitalist reconversion, decisively undermining the image of a strong and homogeneous middle class (Minujin and Kessler 1995; González-Bombal and Svampa 2002; Svampa 2005).

In this period, the "new poor" were identified as middle strata persons whose lowered income left them unable to access necessary basic goods and services (Minujin and López 1994, 94). This situation was the product of an acquired rather than inherited poverty, fostering the characterization of these persons as a "hybrid stratum": close to the middle class in their aspects (small families, educational level) but also to the structural poor in terms of income, unemployment, and job insecurity (Kessler and Di Virgilio 2008). These new poor were forced to change, to adapt to diverse consumption practices, and they lived in heterogeneous spatial distribution (not concentrated in shantytowns). In short, their fall into poverty was the effect of the disappearance of the middle class and not of individual disaffiliation (González-Bombal and Svampa 2002; Kessler and Di Virgilio 2008).

Another core debate simultaneously gained ground. In anthropological literature, the concept of popular sector/class prevailed and went on to designate a heterogeneous set of subaltern groups (industrial workers, informal workers, the unemployed, people assisted by state plans, villagers); they were identified through a combination of political and economic criteria (Semán and Ferraudi-Curto 2016).

To delineate the popular sectors' characterization, Míguez and Semán (2006) identified the recurrence of three categories in these groups' daily social relations: strength, hierarchy, and reciprocity. Strength refers to a physical and moral power associated with a value system. Hierarchy opens a perspective from which to observe, for example, the family dynamics that oscillated between patriarchy and conservatism on the one hand and tentative attempts at equalization and horizontality on the other. It also indicates a way of observing the third category, reciprocity—specifically, the relations of political alliance and the chains of dependencies that it supposes (Miguez and Semán 2006, 27). The crisis in the labor market and "open unemployment" introduced transformations in the cultural matrix of the popular classes: their trajectories were "more uncertain and less promising than what education, work, and progress proposed" (Miguez and Semán 2006, 29; our translation). Difficulties in accessing conventional institutions that allowed an estimation of long-term possibilities instigated the logic of immediate and short-term satisfaction, typical of postwork (and supposedly postclass) societies (Miguez and Semán 2006, 31).

In the years immediately following the 2001 crisis, several authors sought to learn more about how the crisis had impacted the popular class. They investigated the "culture of endurance" (Garriga 2005), musical tastes and styles (Miguez 2006), and popular religiosities (Semán 2006). These authors also captured the revitalization of the territory and the emergence of several organizations and networks oriented toward managing state resources to address poverty (Auyero 2001; Cerrutti and Grimson 2004; Masson 2004; Noel 2006; Quirós 2006). In addition, they introduced the gender perspective in the analysis of social action and political representation and picked up the questions about Peronism, problematizing Germani's perspective once again.

Post-Neoliberalism (2002–2015)

Macroeconomic policy transformations were introduced after Argentina's profound political, economic, and social crisis of 2001–2. These state-promoted changes between 2003 and 2013 implied a return to employment policies that favored the internal market, such as increasing wages, granting subsidies to basic services, and maintaining a competitive exchange rate. These measures had a particular Peronist political stamp that came from their association with the three presidential mandates led by the Kirchners: the first by Néstor from 2003 to 2007 and the second and third by Cristina from 2007 to 2015. The economy grew at an accelerated rate, driven by the expansion of the domestic market and agricultural exports. This cycle, called *post-neoliberal* by the literature (Kessler 2016), pointed to demographic changes: an increase in life expectancy and a decrease in the fertility rate. Social mobility was linked to changing occupations but did not necessarily produce better living conditions, income, or opportunities, particularly for the middle class.

These changes modified the downward trend of the working class, which grew between 2002 and 2010 (with the expansion of job opportunities first in construction and later in the manufacturing sector and associated services). Workers registered with social security once again constituted the dynamic nucleus of the popular class. However, the proportion of the industrial working class was far from the levels reached during the rise of import-substitution industrialization. In addition, urban slums grew (Kessler 2016).

Nevertheless, job insecurity for all wage earners decreased during this period thanks to recovering salaries, expanding consumption, a reactivating economy, and growing job opportunities. The unemployment rate fell (from 17.4 percent to 7.2 percent) with an expansion of the economically active population and the labor market. Salaried and registered workers (with social security coverage) increased, reducing precarious employment (Dalle 2016).

Furthermore, a reduction in class inequality occurred. The most favored were the popular class, whose income increased by around 77 percent between 2003 and 2010. The middle class benefited less, although those with the lowest levels of income in this sector saw the greatest increases. During *relaborization* and the recovery of union activity, the collective path of mobility showed signs of resurgence (Dalle 2016). Workers obtained substantial improvements: generations that had lived through the decline in unionism once again felt they were protagonists in the process of collective social opportunities and improved income.

In this period, only 2.6 percent of middle-class professional/managerial level parents had children who descended into the unskilled popular class. Simultaneously, however, only 2.7 percent of children from the unskilled popular class reached the professional/managerial middle class. Furthermore, 14.1 percent of middle-class children with professional/managerial parents and 21.2 percent of those born to small business owners were inserted into skilled occupations corresponding to the popular classes. Thus, the mobility trends of the middle and popular classes interrupted the polarization process of the 1990s (Benza 2016, 121).

In this period, international organizations and academic literature paid attention to the South American middle classes, demonstrating optimism about post-neoliberalism (Kessler 2016, 23). Their designation as "emerging middle classes," "aspirational middle classes," and "new middle classes" allowed references to be made about a decrease in inequality in the region. In addition to the enormous internal heterogeneity of these classes, their "political stance" was addressed (Kessler 2016, 24): their feared discontent or power of veto was described using various adjectives associated with the ungratefulness and disloyalty they had shown to the governments that had favored them. In Argentina, this reading had little impact: "The keys to our view of the middle class had quite a different intellectual—and structural, I would say—history. First, the quantitative and even political-cultural weight of these social sectors is longstanding, which is why the idea of an emerging middle class did not exist in Argentina in the 1990s. Our debates concerned the impoverishment of the middle sectors" (Kessler 2016, 25; our translation). At the beginning of the twenty-first century, the emerging middle class had a different trajectory in Argentina than in to neighboring countries: the former was composed by social sectors with past histories of decline. They "returned" to positions that once had been consolidated. The disaffection with this history (and the expectation regarding a faster improvement of life and income conditions) had a deep impact during the conflict unleashed by Circular 125 and the subsequent agroexport lockout of 2008.[6] Some authors consider that the circular gave rise to the country's extreme polarization— often referred to as a political *grieta* (crack) (Rodríguez and Touzon 2020) (see part 2).[7] The *grieta* activated the identification between the middle class and the nation. The groups that mobilized against the government—against Peronism and Kirchnerism—were indistinctly characterized as "middle class" but also as the real representatives of a nation that they perceived as white European (Garguín 2013).

In 2015, at the end of the Kirchnerist period, the popular class occupied positions in the Argentine stratification that differed substantially from those of the previous period. The general recovery of employment, wages, and monetary transfer policies modified the reality of households but did not alter the levels of inequity prior to the 2001 crisis (Semán and Ferraudi-Curto 2016, 145). In this context, studies recorded that unlike in previous periods, redistributive social policies benefited not the poorest citizens but employees whose income did not exceed the poverty line, among them "generations that have become impoverished and lost strong insertions in the labor market. People who have moved on from that category and have consolidated a trajectory of intergenerational mobility. People who have started from levels of almost naturalized poverty that they have not been able to transcend. Subjects who have left these situations behind at a crossroads of public policies, personal endeavors, and collective actions. . . . Heads of households who find work is a thinly disguised form of impoverishment" (Semán and Ferraudi-Curto 2016, 151; our translation).

Likewise, the territorial organizational processes for managing public policies persisted but diversified (Semán and Ferraudi-Curto 2016, 156). Toward 2009 a new scenario of convergence between the popular class, the state, and the revitalized unions emerged, including for the first time the collective organization of precarious and informal labor branches. The social positions in the popular-sector world and their wide heterogeneity were the product of their occupational trajectories and the political ties created by the most diverse activism and the state (Semán and Ferraudi-Curto 2016, 162).

Part of the academic, media, and political debate in Argentina attributed to the middle class moral accusations related to their 2015 electoral support for Mauricio Macri's presidential candidacy. But what happened to the popular class? The efforts to answer that question are ongoing and highlight the precarious nature of the well-being granted to the informal workers and a strong crisis in Kirchnerism's public image. These elements were vocalized by middle and popular classes in political-electoral expression (Vomaro and Gené 2017).

Conversely, the analysis of stratification trends in Argentina in the twenty-first century reveals that long-range intergenerational social mobility is an arduous path for members of the popular class because it requires accessing resources to compete in what is still an unequal race that favors those people born in the middle class (Dalle 2016). At least three key factors influence this inequality.

The first is access to education. In recent years, public education—the historically great equalizer of opportunities in Argentina—has deteriorated as a consequence of public policies that have favored coverage over quality (Dalle 2016, 146). Analyses of the relationship between education and social mobility observe that in the twenty-first century, formal education is the main component of (class) occupational achievement in Argentina (Dalle 2016, 155). Class origin maintains its weight "in determining the educational level reached," confirming the inequality of opportunities for children of the middle and popular classes (Dalle 2016, 155; our translation). For people who start out in the same class, education (especially university level) is a central upward mobility mechanism. However, unlike the older generations of the popular class, the youngest are currently seeking shorter tertiary education or university-level courses that "involve less effort in terms of the number of years of study and enable an upward occupational mobility of shorter range" (Dalle 2016, 155; our translation).

The second refers to gender. The massive incorporation of women into the Argentine labor market since the 1970s has enormously transformed social stratification. This phenomenon was linked to several factors: (1) cultural change related to the role of women in society; (2) female educational advancement, with an increase in the opportunity cost for women who chose to stay at home; (3) the expansion of the tertiary sector in the economic structure; (4) the destructuring of the industrialization-development model of import substitution that increased male unemployment and underemployment, reducing wages (Dalle 2016, 156).

The intergenerational social mobility paths taken by women and men from the popular class are different, beyond distinction by age group. The proportion that achieves long-range mobility toward the middle-class faction that has access to capital ownership, authority, and professional expertise is practically the same for both sexes today. However, in the other types of trajectories, the differences are considerable. Women from the popular class tend toward the technical-commercial-administrative segment of the middle class, which involves nonmanual occupational work. Conversely, among men, inheritance or mobility toward the qualified segment of the popular class linked to intergenerational transmission (or through learning a manual trade) predominates. Women tend to stagnate or descend toward the unskilled fraction of the popular class in a considerably higher proportion than men as a result of the female overload of social reproduction and care tasks.

The third is immigration status. According to Dalle (2016), between 1970 and 2013, more than half of the middle class in the Buenos Aires Metropolitan Area had European origins, and many of those families have been living there for one or more generations. The second most important group found in the middle class are descendants of Europeans who rose from the popular class (23.9 percent) (Dalle 2016). Third-generation people of European origin represent 33.5 percent of the middle class; 16 percent moved up from the popular class, and 17.5 percent remained stable in the middle class. The contribution of families with a Latin American migrant origin to the middle class amounts to 10 percent (6.1 percent have come from the popular class) (Dalle 2016).

Between 1970 and 2013, 52.5 percent of popular-class families of European migratory origin reached middle-class positions. Internal migrants and the ones from neighboring countries enter through the lower social strata but usually ascend gradually in mobility, although they face sociocultural barriers imposed by racist criteria (Dalle 2016). Immigrants from neighboring countries also have lower chances of intergenerational occupational advancement than do Argentines born in the Buenos Aires Metropolitan Area and migrants from other regions of the country who have the same occupational origin and the same educational achievements.

To summarize, the descendants of Europeans whose parents were from the popular class experienced greater upward social mobility than people who came from families with three or more generations of Argentines or who are Latin American migrants and their descendants. In a society with a Europeanizing social imaginary, prejudice and stigmatization act as obstacles to mestizo Argentine families' social mobility and those of Latin American migratory origin (especially if they have Indigenous or African ancestry) (Dalle 2016).

Part 2 illustrates how several of the debates synthesized in this chapter are embodied in the concrete experience of a working-class man, Ramiro.

Part 2. The Case Study

Chapter Four

The Ethnographic Approach

Narrating Trajectories, Extending Ethnography

In chapter 1, we mentioned that the case study that gave rise to this book relied on ethnographic methodology. However, it is important to qualify that statement: we understand ethnography as the systematic observation of social contexts with the aim of participating in them, recording and analyzing them, and building narratives from them. An ethnographic methodological perspective seeks a critical interaction between the subjects of study and researchers: it is an approach, a method, and an intersubjective exercise in storytelling (Guber 2001, 12). There are many different ways of carrying out an ethnographic study, and we used the Extended Case Method (ECM), also known as situational analysis.

Developed by Max Gluckman and his followers at the Manchester School of Anthropology and Sociology in the first half of the twentieth century, the ECM initially drew on ethnographic studies on the processes of colonization, migration, urbanization, and racial conflicts in Africa (Frankenberg 2006). One of Gluckman's main theoretical-methodological debates was with his former professor Bronisław Malinowski, who was then considered the founder of the modern ethnographic methodology. In his efforts to refute Malinowski, Gluckman created an anthropological theory of conflict and social change and proposed a new set of ethnographic narrative techniques. According to Gluckman, the hegemony of Malinowski's method had culminated in a limited narrative use of ethnographic cases, which he referred to as the "method of apt illustration":

We made a large number of observations on how subjects actually behaved, we collected genealogies and censuses, made diagrams of villages and gardens, listened to cases and quarrels, obtained commentaries on all those incidents, collected texts from informants about customs and rituals, and discovered their answer to "cases stated." Out of this vast mass of data we analyzed a general outline of the culture, or the social system according to our main theoretical bent. We then used the apt and appropriate case to illustrate specific customs, principles of organization, social relations, etc. Each case was selected for its appropriateness at a particular point in the argument; and cases coming close together in the argument might be derived from actions or words of quite different groups or individuals. (Gluckman 2006 [1961], 15)

The problem of such uses resides in the fact that the theoretical map ultimately imposed severe limitations on empirical information, even when the research centered on the complexity of groups and their social life—thus extrapolating the folklorist reductionism of the description of customs so common to anthropological narratives before Malinowski. In other words, the theoretical model on the social function of institutions oriented the bricolage of the example. These are viewed as illustrative of what was previously postulated in theoretical terms. This emphasis on the reproductive aspect of social life would progressively render invisible the very processes that were the object of study, preventing correlations between the different cases and inhibiting the understanding of the profound and diachronic relationship observed in social situations (Gluckman 2006 [1961], 15).

This is one of the reasons why Gluckman's proposal is a contribution for those of us interested in narrating people's vital transformations. His point is simple: Malinowski's use of narrative stories deforms the historicity of social phenomenon. Yet where does one begin to change this perspective?

According to Gluckman (2006 [1961]), the change starts with altering the way we anthropologists narrate and work with the stories from field diaries: an understanding of social life as a process implies observing and experiencing different social situations and then describing and cataloging them separately as different cases. Observation is centered on interacting with the conflict to conduct a situational analysis of how each group of people (or each person) situates themselves. The key, then, lies in building extensive narratives of these conflicts, linking them to historical processes and specific contexts (Frankenberg 2006, 203–4). The central methodological point is the political dimension of the narrative structure in the social sciences. Thus, the ECM proposes to redirect Malinowski's methodology (Burawoy 1998, 6) with the clear aim of introducing a new anthropological narrative (Frankenberg 2006, 206–7).

In summary, at least three aspects of the ECM distinguish it from classic ethnographic approaches. First, it involves a particular way of treating empirical ethnographic material. As opposed to citing ethnographic examples to deductively illustrate analytical and theoretical perspectives, Gluckman proposed "to turn this relationship between the case and statement on its head" (Evens and Handelman 2006, 1), selecting ethnographic scenes and narrating them sequentially. Second, ECM is developed through the study of social interactions with the potential for conflict (Gluckman 2006 [1961], 17).[1] Third, it targets a diachronic understanding of social situations, identifying the historical processes that influence everyday experience in order to forge interdisciplinary ties with historical studies for the reconstruction of the macroeconomic, social, and political contexts (Gluckman 2006 [1961]).

In this case study, we bring all three of these points into play. We offer an example of how the sequential narrative of a life trajectory's outcomes can be used to identify analytical knots that can be researched and theorized. Using experimental writing, we present an exercise in extending ethnography. The reconstruction of Ramiro's narrative about his personal and family history considers these inferences. By choosing this reconstruction, we also address the relationships among life histories, conditioning, positions, and class situations, overcoming what Bourdieu (1977, 82) referred to as the "biographical illusion": the methodological-analytical aberration of considering a subject confined to an atomized, ahistorical, individualist existence. This motivates our emphasis on specifically reconstructing class conflicts, focusing on those scenes or stories that denote strife between different social groups in San Telmo. In operative terms, we utilized three methodological tools.

First, we carried out ethnographic observations recorded in field diaries and photographs between August 2019 and March 2020. This chapter and chapter 5 draw heavily on these observations, which proved fundamental for adequately contextualizing Ramiro's stories in and about San Telmo.

Second, we conducted a quantitative survey with ten people. The survey design was based on the core topics and questions of Argentina's National Social Structure Survey conducted by the Research Program on Contemporary Argentine Society. The questionnaire comprised of eighty-one questions, divided into seven sections: (1) Housing and Habitat, (2) Mobilities and Identity Labels, (3) Infringement of Rights, (4) Diet and Nutrition, (5) Access to Goods, Services, and Assistance from Others, (6) Household Income, and (7) Self-Identified Social Class. The results of the survey were not the main input of this study, but they did serve as a starting point: we used interviewees' responses to draft a summary of how San Telmo residents and workers classify the neighborhood.

Third, we conducted life history interviews with ten people (five men and five women). A digital voice recorder was used for the interviews, which were then transcribed for analysis.[2] In the process of interpreting the material, we selected individuals whose trajectories revealed an accumulation of macrosocial processes that affect or shape class conflicts in the neighborhood. Ramiro's interview, conducted in February 2020, was the first of these.

San Telmo, an Old Neighborhood

In addition to being one of the city's oldest neighborhoods, San Telmo was the site of one of the first settlements in Buenos Aires. During colonial times, it was known as Los Altos de San Pedro Telmo (the Heights of San Pedro Telmo) because it was a port neighborhood located on the hills overlooking the Río de la Plata shore. Products brought in by ship from other cities located in modern-day Argentina, Paraguay, and Uruguay were traded and sold in the neighborhood. In fact, the international tourist attraction known as the Mercado de San Telmo occupies the same spot where an outdoor market existed four centuries ago. The current roofed structure was built in 1897 as the neighborhood underwent major transformations. For centuries after the Spanish colony was established, San Telmo was an enclave for Buenos Aires's elites, but at the end of the nineteenth century, it gradually evolved into a working-class neighborhood due to the arrival of a wave of migrants (Malfa 2004, 32–33).

A series of landfills created along the river and urban transformations to the city's south side mean that the neighborhood is no longer close to the water. However, it has not lost its port identity or its bohemian air, both of which are part of the local imaginary, and it remains home to tango dance halls and numerous bars. In terms of administrative divisions, San Telmo is part of District 1, a border between the downtown area of the city of Buenos Aires and the neighborhoods that make up the city's southern strip (Grimberg 2009, 84).[3]

San Telmo is officially bordered by the neighborhoods of Monserrat to the north (up to Chile Street), Puerto Madero to the east (up to Ingeniero Huergo Avenue), La Boca to the southeast (up to Paseo Colón Avenue), Barracas to the southwest (up to Caseros Avenue), and Constitución to the west (up to Piedras Street) (map 1). Yet within the imaginaries of the neighborhood's residents, these definitions often prove problematic. As Girola, Yacovino, and Laborde (2011, 29–32) have noted, renewed interest in San Telmo as a tourist attraction since the 1990s have led nearby residents and merchants to claim the places where they live, shop, and work as part of San Telmo even when they technically lie outside the neighborhood's boundaries.

In general terms, San Telmo has a solid public transport system and good services and is well connected, though it is plagued by historical housing infrastructure issues and overcrowding. At the same time, it is a historic district with many protected buildings. In addition to making San Telmo a tourist attraction, the architecture gives these streets a visual and social identity that distinguishes them from other neighborhoods on the south side of Buenos Aires

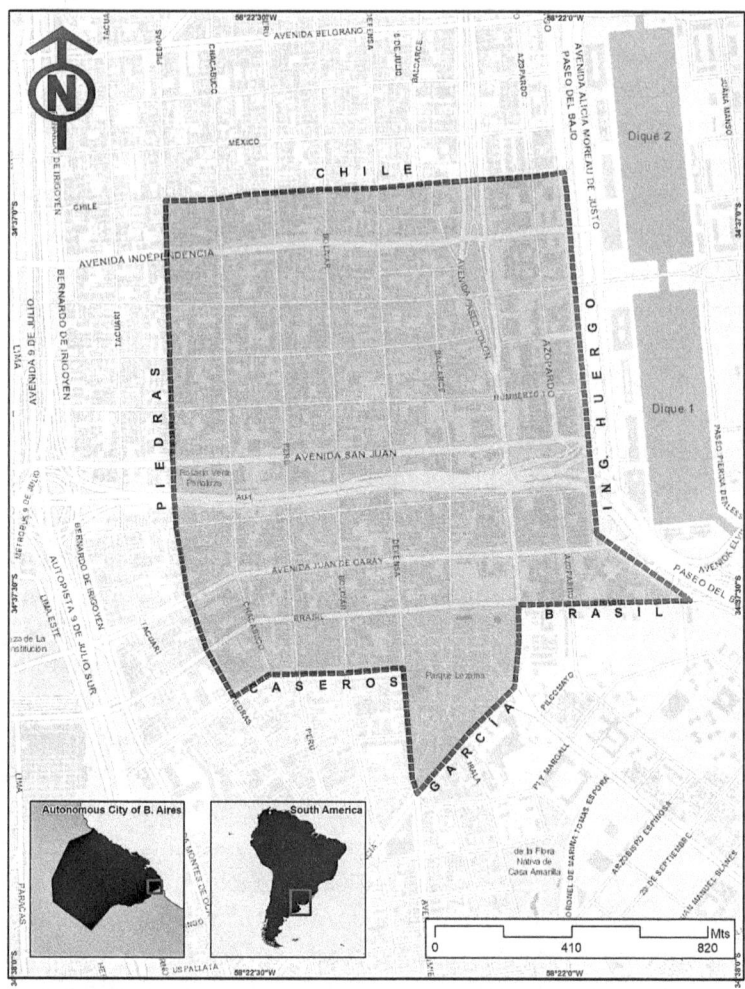

The neighborhood's location in the Autonomous City of Buenos Aires (CABA), Argentina. Source: created by Paulo Contreras Osses for the PICT Project 2017-1767.

(Girola, Yacovino, and Laborde 2011, 29) (photographs 2–4). San Telmo is also home to a dense network of trade unions, social organizations, and community movements: an organized social fabric that is a benchmark for other neighborhoods in the city (photographs 5–6).

A scene from the traditional antiques and crafts market that has spilled over the streets of San Telmo every Sunday since the seventies and is one of the main tourist attractions in the city. San Telmo (CABA, Argentina). September 2019. Photographer: Menara Guizardi.

Our quantitative and qualitative results allowed us to sketch out three core thematic areas of the neighborhood during the crisis between the end of 2019 and the beginning of 2020. We remained in touch with our collaborators even after Argentina ordered its lockdown in mid-March 2020. Through their stories, we are aware that the social, human, and food-related crises in the neighborhood have only worsened since the onset of the COVID-19 pandemic. In this regard, all indicators point to a much more severe crisis in the near future. The descriptions we obtained at the beginning of 2020 can help us understand these outcomes but must also be seen as representative of a continually shifting context.

First, residents perceive great diversity in the neighborhood's social stratification. In their view, the coexistence of different social classes is both an identifying feature of the neighborhood and a constitutive element of its history. They note, for example, that neighborhood residents include those "with plenty of *guita* [money]"—professors, artists, foreigners, and workers—but San Telmo is also a favorite spot for the informal street vendors who visit

This image shows inside the original building of San Telmo's Traditional Market. Considered one of the oldest trading places in the city, it dates from the Colony in the seventeenth century. The current construction dates from the nineteenth century and houses various stalls where fruits, vegetables, meats, bread, and various services used to be sold. Nowadays, these stands are filled with antiques, cafes, crafts, "ethnic" products, and gourmet restaurants aimed at tourists. San Telmo (CABA, Argentina). September 2019. Photographer: Menara Guizardi.

the neighborhood daily (photographs 7–8). Residents associate this diversity with different stages of the neighborhood's history, noting how it received mainly working-class European migrants (especially Italians and Spaniards) between the end of the nineteenth century and the first half of the twentieth century (photograph 9). The neighborhood subsequently received internal migrants from several provinces—Salta and Tucumán are the two most frequently mentioned—in the 1970s and 1980s. The San Telmo residents interviewed also mention the arrival of migrants from neighboring countries (Uruguayans, Bolivians, and Paraguayans) starting in the 1980s, with Colombians and Venezuelans arriving since 2016.

When residents were asked to classify San Telmo, most dismissed the survey's options and instead offered a new category, "a hybrid."[4] On the one hand, it is a slum, giving the current and historical presence of the poor and members of the working class who

The Heritage buildings on Perú street, where the hustle and bustle of the fast-living neighborhood can be seen. San Telmo (CABA, Argentina). February 2020. Photographer: Menara Guizardi.

live in overcrowded homes, squats, *conventillos* (collective residences shared by poor families), and run-down motels in addition to a significant number of homeless people who live or spend time on the neighborhood streets. The high homeless population can be attributed to the multiple, dense networks that provide assistance—privately run soup kitchens, social and political organizations—in San Telmo and its location as a point of contact between the city's

Members of a community social organization known as the San Telmo Popular Assembly block an avenue in the neighborhood protesting against evictions from social housing. San Telmo (CABA, Argentina). February 2020. Photographer: Menara Guizardi.

San Telmo's neighbors cut off the street protesting against the repeated power cuts during the summer. In the background, the heritage buildings of "El Federal" stand out. This historical cafeteria from the nineteenth century is one of the neighborhood's tourist attractions. San Telmo (CABA, Argentina). January 2020. Photographer: Menara Guizardi.

San Telmo (CABA, Argentina). September 2019.
Photographer: Menara Guizardi.

San Telmo (CABA, Argentina). September 2019.
Photographer: Menara Guizardi.

Don Eduardo, a shoemaker of Spanish origin, arrived in San Telmo when he was still a baby, his parents having been displaced by the conflicts after the Spanish Civil War. In the picture, he fixes a shoe in the store he inherited from his father. In the background, a sign protesting against the gentrification of the Mercado del Barrio. San Telmo (CABA, Argentina). November 2019. Photographer: Menara Guizardi.

downtown and the neighborhoods along the southern strip. Based on these features, San Telmo can be characterized as an urban zone of transition.[5]

Our interviewees also stated that the neighborhood is a fully urban settlement, with sidewalks and sewers, given the presence of middle- and upper-class sectors in "the good houses and buildings" (in the words of one interviewee) and the reurbanization of public spaces in the twenty-first century as part of the neighborhood's transformation into a strategic site for international tourism (and the businesses associated with it, such as restaurants, bars, hotels, stores, antique shops). All of this gives the neighborhood a certain air of social distinction.

Second, based on the interviews, the social picture that takes shape is one of a growing crisis in San Telmo. According to those who run the neighborhood's soup kitchens, the demand for food has increased exponentially since 2019. In January 2020, when public schools were closed for the summer vacation, the demand from parents looking to feed their school-age children exceeded what the local soup kitchens had to offer. According to the manager of one of these soup kitchens, the requests for bag lunches and food increased 150 percent that month. Soup kitchen staff talked to us about a crisis in the care this population receives and reported referring families to city, provincial, and national welfare services. They also had discovered that several families started visiting the soup kitchen because they had recently fallen below the poverty line and were sleeping on the streets for the first time in their lives. This reveals the surprising shift of family units that perceived themselves as working-class or lower-middle-class into extreme poverty (because one or both of the adults had lost their jobs and been unable to find alternative income).

During the interviews, a second vulnerable group was mentioned: older people. The stories describe impoverished diets and worsening housing conditions for the neighborhood's older adults, who also represent a significant percentage of those whose income has fallen in recent years. According to the leaders of the social organizations we interviewed, the food crisis these groups suffer is as bad or worse than what they suffered during the 2001 crisis.

Neighborhood residents, merchants, and social/political organizations reacted differently to this social crisis. While certain local merchants had begun contributing to volunteer networks providing food—spending one workday handing out free food to neighborhood residents—others felt the crisis was more of a public security issue. These interviewees noted a rise in petty crime on the neighborhood streets and associated it with the social crisis. Based on this assumption, some merchants added that the rise in robberies scared off tourists and dampened economic activities. They wanted more local police on the streets. We can thus see how the process of local impoverishment is interpreted as a security problem, establishing a framework for understanding in which a socioeconomic

Young people coordinate the Darío Santillán *Community Dining Room, which gives snacks and provides school support to the neighborhood's children in the afternoons. The dining room is one example of the community's self-managed organizations linked to the San Telmo Popular Assembly. San Telmo (CABA, Argentina). February 2020. Photographer: Menara Guizardi.*

condition (poverty) is juxtaposed with crime. This imaginary informed the political stances of middle-class sectors in the neighborhood whose livelihood depended on tourism or commerce.

The third area of analytical reflections in the San Telmo case study is related to the strong female role in local social organizations, particularly in those providing support for the lower-middle-class population suffering from gradual impoverishment (soup kitchens, housing committees) (photograph 10).

Women have promoted and developed social networks that attempt to offset, with varying degrees of success, the myriad shortfalls associated with the reduction in health, education, and cultural services and the negative aspects of the rise in unemployment. Though this is not a new phenomenon, it is a critical ethnographic datum for understanding the gender dimensions of these processes in San Telmo. Among the women interviewed, those in leading roles were also the heads of their households and were responsible for domestic work in their homes. Thus, the leading social reproduction role they took on as carers within their families expanded into a similar role in community care. At the same time, their leadership was part of territorializing the political representation of popular sectors and had important effects on public space within the neighborhood. For example, in the second week of February 2020, we observed a roadblock protest on Independencia Avenue coordinated by female leaders in the neighborhood. The protest was organized because a children's soup kitchen headed by a group of four young women was being threatened with eviction.

The interviews with these women reveal their awareness of the productive/reproductive, personal/community, and social/political burden on their shoulders. This burden is part of the self-perceived traits that define their class role. In other words, these women understood that their class identities—lower-middle-class or working class—were strongly tied to their many social and family obligations and that in a circular process, their gender identity is precisely where these burdens originate.

Ramiro, the main character in our case study, was a social actor who represented the neighborhood's diversity as well as the tensions and conflicts between subjects who see themselves as part of a shared environment but not necessarily as part of a community, as Weber (1978 [1922]) reflected. Ramiro's story helps us reconstruct a fractional, situated history of these class conflicts.

Chapter Five

Ramiro

From Tucumán to Buenos Aires

Ramiro was born in 1957 to Valentina Carmen after a very difficult home birth. At that time, his family lived in a small town in the province of San Miguel de Tucumán (popularly known as Tucumán) in the Noroeste Argentino (Argentine Northwest, NOA).[1]

Those born in NOA assume a very particular place in the symbolic hierarchies and otherness that have laid the groundwork for the country's imagined community. Political centralization of the Argentine state marginalizes the country's border zones and renders them invisible, especially those farthest from Buenos Aires (Karasic 1994, 7–10). Symbolically, this marginalization exceeds geographical distances and extends to the ethnic makeup of border territories like those found in NOA, where a significant number of diverse native ethnic groups dwell.[2] In the configuration of national identity discourses, most of which are produced in the capital city of Buenos Aires, these groups—and even their territories—have been made invisible (Karasic 2000, 153).[3] This accompanies the construction of "racist mythomanias" that depict Argentina as a country whose population comes from Europe (Grimson 2012, 27), as discussed in chapter 3.

Therefore, despite Tucumán's importance in the country's history and national politics (Argentina declared its independence from Spain at an 1816 congress in the province's capital city), Ramiro's home province is a peripheral territory. His origins there influenced his trajectory, especially after his arrival to Buenos Aires, where he was identified as Indigenous, Black, or Morocho, classifications that did not necessarily correspond to those assigned to him in his hometown. At home, his mother and siblings referred to him as Indian, but from his perspective, this was a generic term of affection: it was completely normal for everyone to call each other that. Ramiro was not sure whether he had Indigenous ancestors.

A specific incident led Ramiro to migrate to Buenos Aires. As he recalled,

The thing is, we suffered a lot in Tucumán. Because I lost my dad when I was thirteen. And since my father had been the sole breadwinner, and there were seven of us, we had a tough time. We went hungry, and that's when we had to split up, each off to seek their destiny. But I had a terrible time of it. I only made it to seventh grade [of primary school]. My siblings, too; none of them made it past seventh grade. I started working at the age of thirteen. . . . In my first job, I looked after fighting cocks for rich people: police chiefs, lawyers. Then my brother's brother-in-law showed up and got me a job at a builder's yard. I worked my fingers to the bone in that job. They sell iron, cement, sand, limestone, bricks at the builder's yard, you know? I carried sugar. I was 62 kilos [146 pounds] and loaded sugar bags that weighed 73 kilos [161 pounds]. I was really skinny, but the guys helped me; they taught me. I carried the cement that came from Santiago del Estero, boiling hot. We'd put a rag on. Sometimes I put the rag up top [on the head]. I was so skinny because I wasn't eating enough. A thousand, two thousand, three thousand of those bags. I suffered there. . . . Later, my brother was working as a plumber in a neighborhood. I started plumbing and learned the trade.[4]

The productive and reproductive burden on his mother and his father's death led to situations that would shape Ramiro and his siblings' trajectories, closing off certain possibilities to them (continuing their education, for example). This forced them to accept precarious work, "in whatever was going," jobs where "they worked their fingers to the bone."

As discussed in chapter 3, during the 1970s, young Argentine men from popular sectors had to acquire certain social capital to get work: opportunities came through networks and family ties (generally the men). Learning a trade—the cultural capital necessary for doing the work—was also facilitated by men from the family networks or male coworkers. Through these trades, Ramiro experienced a "short-range upward mobility" (Pla 2017, 3; our translation), going from an unskilled informal worker to a skilled self-employed worker. Those years of hardship led family members to migrate in search of better incomes. In 1977, "I came here [to Buenos Aires] and worked as a plumber; that's how I made a living. I was twenty when I got here. I came by myself to visit my mom. Because my mom and my older sister had already moved here to live. My mom dedicated her life to her children until she was forty-four—that's the kind of mother I had. She raised us until we were grown up."

Ramiro's family difficulties were part of a set of problems that affected the inhabitants of Argentina's rural peripheral areas. In the mid-twentieth century, scant state investment in these areas had yielded high levels of poverty and increasingly precarious work (mostly rural) (Caggiano 2007, 95). Thus, these territories played a major role in the country's abrupt rural-urban migration between 1930 and 1980 (see chapter 3). Different dynamics and moments characterized this migration over the decades and ultimately transformed the demographic-territorial structure in less than half a century.[5]

Nevertheless, the migration experience of Ramiro's family has an important gender dimension. The women entrusted with social reproduction within the family (his mother and older sister) are the ones who migrated to the capital in search of wages to improve the family unit's economic conditions. Urban transition is an abrupt phenomenon and one that took place across Latin America from 1930 to 1990. Androcentric readings of this process tend to overlook the central role women like Ramiro's mother and sister play in the countryside as well as the role they play in communal spaces of the poor urban neighborhoods where they arrived. In these realms, women's strategies prove critical, structuring new ideas and practices on social reproduction, entry to the workforce, solidarity, communities, and families (Guizardi, Gonzálvez and Stefoni 2018). Ramiro's mother dedicated herself exclusively to these tasks until she was forty-four, a late age considering she married and had her first child at sixteen. Thus, being a single mother, combined with the lack of public social protection systems to alleviate the burden, is connected to the precarious employment of sons and daughters, given their limited schooling (an institutionalized cultural capital) and rural-urban migration flows.

The abandonment of the countryside in favor of the capital city coincided with a mass of European migrants from different countries (most of whom had arrived between 1870 and 1930) and their descendants. Together, they formed an industrial army reserve (Margulis 1977). They also shared San Telmo and other working-class residential enclaves on the south side of Buenos Aires.[6] However, there were substantial identity-related differences between these migrants. Although they frequently held the same jobs and worked in the same sectors as the international migrants, the internal ones were viewed as racially inferior not only by the elites but also by foreign workers and *porteños* (those born in Buenos Aires). This inferiority is captured in the derogatory and stigmatizing term *cabecitas negras* (a polysemic concept that derogatorily alludes to people with different shades of brown skin and dark hair) (Grimson 2012, 27). Although they did get somewhat involved in the intense union activity that characterized life in Buenos Aires starting in the first half of the twentieth century (Cattaruzza 2019), the immigrants and migrants had different opportunities for social mobility and trajectories marked by racial differentiations and different urban housing spaces, as explained in chapter 3. Even within working-class neighborhoods, these groups occupied separate enclaves.

The large presence of these internal migrants in the capital city elicited a range of political and social reactions on the part of the elites, who clung to racist ideologies that inextricably tied the nation's progress to the whiteness of its population (Germani 2010 [1962], 493). This denigration took on particular political meanings beginning on October 17, 1945, with the massive march to defend Juan Domingo Perón in Buenos Aires. That day, the hordes of both internal and international migrants brought about an identity clash that would change the country's political semantics: "The *porteños*—who established society proud to inhabit a cosmopolitan, white, European city—found themselves faced by the unknown. Astonishment, shame, hatred, indignation, compassion, disinterest, sadness, and fear are some of the emotions that were expressed. The sheer number of people meant, at the very least, the total breakdown of daily life. In this unprecedented event, real-life crowds ran into deep-rooted imagination" (Grimson 2019, 61; our translation).

On the days that followed, the Argentine papers began to build a discourse in which these popular sectors were described by a battery of disparaging terms: "hordes, mobs, masses, the tribe, workers, *lumpenproletariat, malevaje* [riffraff], *malón* [Indian raiders], *chusma* [unrefined], *descamisados* [the shirtless], Blacks or *alpargatas* [espadrilles, common footwear of the poor]" (Grimson 2019, 62; our translation). Slowly, an imaginary took shape in which elite political sectors combined class labels ("workers," "*descamisados,*" "*pies descalzos*" [the barefooted]) with racial ("*cabecitas negras*") and political ones ("Peronists") (Grimson 2019, 61–65; our translation).

Grimson (2019, 61) has shown how Argentina refused to acknowledge the existence of Indians, African Argentines, and mestizos, who were thus also denied the right to belong to the city's central spaces. This refusal laid the groundwork for a strong political structure and contributed to the polarization between hegemonic political stances (a *grieta*, as explained in chapters 1 and 3). Despite the complexity and diversity involved, it boils down to the long-lasting and constantly renewed symbolic dichotomy between Peronists and anti-Peronists. This structure replicates the logic of racial opposition between whites and nonwhites. Consequently, it is impossible to understand class differentiation and "Argentine politics without analyzing the constitutive role" of racism (Grimson 2019, 53–54; our translation).

This *grieta* is responsible for erasing or hiding those who are not considered white enough to be "Argentine." This logic has a particular urban character in Buenos Aires, structuring the city's internal borders and limits. The story of Ramiro, who continues to be identified as Black by some of his neighbors, illustrates this juxtaposition of racial hierarchy, political identity, and the right to access the city within a specific trajectory and neighborhood context.

The Tucumán Enclave of San Telmo

Ramiro initially planned to stay in Buenos Aires for just a few days but changed his plans: "I didn't come to live in Buenos Aires: I came to visit my mom. And on that Sunday, I was scheduled to go back—I already had the ticket—I met the woman I would marry. I met her. I stayed, I never used the ticket, I gave up everything. Then she got pregnant, and here's what happened: we rented a room here on block 500 of Estados Unidos [a San Telmo street]. We had nothing to our names, absolutely nothing. A young man from Tucumán who was living in a *conventillo* gave me a bed, a mattress. It's still there, and it's still a *conventillo*."

Ramiro migrated for love in circumstances that were very different from those of many other Tucumán residents who left between 1975 and 1977. They left as a result of Operativo Independencia (Operation Independence), a province-wide state of siege and widespread military repression against anyone viewed as "subversive" (Garaño 2016, 6). The armed forces were sent into Tucumán, where several clandestine centers of torture and forced disappearance operated, leading to the murder of countless political opponents. The difficulties of living under state terrorism led to a mass exodus from Tucumán to the province of Buenos Aires. Without mentioning these events, Ramiro explains that his migration was not tied to this historical process.

When Ramiro's partner became pregnant, they had to find a place where they could be comfortable with a child. San Telmo was the most accessible option. The neighborhood was built during colonial times in the sixteenth century and was the enclave of Buenos Aires's aristocratic elites until well into the twentieth century. Outbreaks of yellow fever in 1852, 1858, 1870, and 1871 drastically reduced the city's population and particularly that of San Telmo. Elites gradually began moving to the north side of Buenos Aires, initiating the urbanization of an area that still had enormous houses and gardens where social distancing was possible even into the 1920s (Ursino 2012).[7]

Toward the end of the decade, the enormous colonial mansions of San Telmo were split up into living quarters for several families and rented out (Ursino 2012), with the families sharing a patio, a bathroom, and in some cases a kitchen—a type of tenement known in Argentina as *conventillo*. This was the principal housing solution for the families of international migrants and, from the 1930s onward, of internal migrants as well. Thus, the neighborhood suffered a process of *déclassement* (declassification) and *reclassement* (reclassification).

In *conventillos*, migrants did not have to present any legal guarantees to rent a room: the rooms were small but boasted a central location, thus facilitating access to better-paid jobs and reducing transport costs. Ramiro and his partner moved to one in 1977. According to him, people chose their *conventillo* based on their origin: areas within the neighborhood were divided regionally. Estados Unidos Street was an enclave for migrants from the NOA, with "more than a dozen *conventillos*" for migrants from Tucumán and Salta. The networks of families and others who hailed from one's hometown allowed the new residents to get to know the landlords, rent a room, and get furniture.

Ramiro explained that the location of the tenement house proved critical to getting work as a plumber. At the end of the 1970s, urban interventions were rampant in San Telmo as part of General Jorge Rafael Videla's military regime's (1976–81) plans to control the capital city (Oszlak 1991). The state expropriated and tore down some homes dating back to colonial times to build several major avenues (Independencia, San Juan, and Juan de Garay) and connect the city via highway to Greater Buenos Aires (Girola, Yacovino, and Laborde 2011).[8] During this process, authorization was granted to build several residential towers on the newly empty lots (Girola, Yacovino, and Laborde 2011). This increased the neighborhood's population density and the availability of new housing aimed at self-employed professionals or civil servants, who could walk to their downtown offices.

Yet these new buildings did not replace the *conventillos* or force their residents out: the two worlds formed a working relationship. The people from the tenements—the popular sectors—found work as doormen, building superintendents, plumbers, masons, and domestic employees for the new middle-class residents. The neighborhood, however, continued to diversify. Along with the European and internal migrants, migrants from Uruguay, Paraguay, and Bolivia began moving into the remaining tenements. Overcrowding and a rise in criminal activity gave the neighborhood a particular stigma:

> It was a terrible place. San Telmo was full of *conventillos*, which, in turn, were full of thieves. There were a lot of drugs, too. Right there, across that street where that building is [on Peru Street], there was a *conventillo*. There were so many thieves, so many drugs. The streetwalkers, all young girls, hung out until the sun came up at a café that used to be there on the corner. There were two bars: one on the corner and the other a bit farther down. Plus, the guys would pull up and get out of their cars with what they had stolen. We used to eat there, you know? These guys would come in with stuff they had stolen—they knew the owner. They'd unload their loot, and then fights would ensue—guns, knives, anything went. It was a disaster. There were a lot of Uruguayans. And then the Peruvians started arriving. Things were messed up here in San Telmo. It was a disaster. Things got a lot better when they removed the *conventillos*. There's one of them that still rents rooms—the only one left is on this block [on Estados Unidos Street].

From the end of the 1970s onward, the neighborhood became known as a space inhabited by members of multiple social sectors. The groups that came together drew on heterogeneous references used to identify others, labeling people based on their labor insertion, job status, gender, national origin, or, among the Argentines, province of origin. There were European migrants (and their descendants), internal migrants, and migrants from neighboring countries; wage workers and small shop owners; artists; muggers, traffickers, and sex workers; liberal professionals and self-employed businesspeople; civil servants; and the occasional former aristocrat fallen on bad times without enough money to move to the north side of the city.

This heterogeneity was expressed in the relational uses of public space. In the common areas of the neighborhood—squares, corners, streets, restaurants, and cafés—personal interactions took on an adaptive, functional coexistence. In the same places where workers had lunch, traffickers sold their products, prostitutes met clients, and thieves divvied up their daily earnings. To each their own. This articulating logic of heterogeneity coexisted with segregation logics that affected residential spaces that were separated according to the origins of their inhabitants.

However, the living and public spaces had one cross-cutting trait: in both, racial stereotypes were employed as dialogue markers between the neighborhood's different groups. Tucumán natives, for example, suffered mistreatment at workplaces and in relationships with coworkers. Colleagues used the stigmatizing *cabecitas negras* to remind them of their subordinate position. Ramiro found a surprising way of avoiding this, adopting an "extremely passive" stance at work that, in his telling, prevented others from calling him Black and helped him avoid the problem:

> I was never mistreated, not me, but others were. But not me because I'm an extremely passive guy. [Tucumán migrants living in San Telmo] would get into fights with people when they went to work. They were mistreated. But everyone treated me well. . . . I only suffered discrimination here on one occasion, but it wasn't anything serious: someone called me Black. But I didn't get upset because I am Black. I am Morocho. It doesn't bother me if someone calls me Black: it's the same to me; it doesn't affect me. It doesn't affect me. What do I know? I don't get upset. No, I don't pay attention to stuff like that. I'm not interested: they can call me whatever they like, but I just don't answer. But I know that in the café [on the corner], this dark-skinned guy got into a fight with a white guy. And when I got there, punches were flying because the guy had called him a *negro de mierda* [shitty Black].

Ramiro recounts that police abuse on the neighborhood streets responds—and has always responded—to this racialized logic. "Police are always abusive. For example, not too long ago, they stopped two dark-skinned guys. They asked them to show some identification, but the guys didn't have their IDs on them. So they threw them down on the ground, stomped on their heads, their arms. There were like three cop cars. I have no idea what the guys had done, but you can't treat them like that. So what do I know? I didn't like that. But what could I do? Start yelling? I'd end up in jail."

"Ending up in jail" has a transcendent meaning: his use of this expression indicates that Ramiro is also seen as a Morocho and thus at risk of getting arrested without any legal justification. His "passive" strategy is an important mechanism, one he developed as a young man to circumvent the structural violence that stems from inequalities and denying rights to workers considered Black or "Morocho.[9]

In addition to adopting a strategically passive attitude toward the building superintendents who called on him for plumbing services, Ramiro inverts the meaning of the terms of identity *Black* and *Morocho* in a strong symbolic appropriation. Therefore, he reformulates these terms to strip them of their derogatory meaning. In his story, he associates these two processes to his religious conversion from nonbeliever to Christian. Going to services at an Evangelical church led him to adopt the habits of the "good life" the pastors recommend: no drinking, no smoking, no drugs. To a certain extent, this choice means that his employers see him as serene, a good worker, and "strongly disciplined." "That's why they love me so much." Thus, his passiveness, ability to reformulate the meaning of insults, and strong discipline make Ramiro "well-loved." Yet not everyone in the neighborhood agrees with this strategy. In the public spaces of San Telmo, there is a limit to how many racial slurs a person can hear without resorting to conflict, as in the scene in the bar.

From Informal to Formal

Settled in the enclave "of Tucumán natives," Ramiro and his partner had three sons and one daughter. For eighteen years, they lived in different *conventillos* in the neighborhood. His wife looked after the house and children and worked as a housekeeper. He worked as a plumber in different homes as well as in the building where he is now the superintendent. The owners of the apartments soon got to know him and "trusted his work." In 1995, the building administrator—an accountant hired by the residents—invited Ramiro, then age thirty-eight, to become the building superintendent. That has been his main job ever since. The building is located on one of the neighborhood's main streets, just two blocks from the San Telmo market and three from Defensa Street, where the tourist fair is held every Sunday. A solid example of the unique *porteño* take on rationalism, the building dates from the 1940s. It has two blocks, each eight stories high. The first block has twenty-eight apartments and the second thirty-two, for a total of sixty. The building entrance features a heavy iron and glass door that leads to the reception area, with a counter for the superintendent to work behind and an area with sofas and a coffee table. The elevator for the first block is to the left, and a staircase is off to the side. Behind the reception area is an enormous patio filled with plants. A hallway running past the patio leads to the ground-floor apartments and the elevator for the second block. Farther back is another large garden with trees, a fountain, and flowers, an open-air space within the city block shared by several buildings.

As is customary in older buildings in Buenos Aires, an apartment is reserved for the superintendent. Ramiro's apartment is on the ground floor next to the stairwell leading up to the apartments in the front block. Measuring approximately fifty square meters, it has a small kitchen with a dining area, where a circular table sits with four chairs. It has a decent-sized bedroom that opens onto the building's common green areas, a bathroom, and another small bedroom that Ramiro uses for storage. This is where he came to live with his partner and children. He originally had an informal employment arrangement—no contract, no social security, no health or accident insurance—until he finally got a regular labor contract in 2000. "I was lucky," he says: not only because it was his first work contract at forty-three and he had given up hope on getting one but also because Argentina was in the throes of one of the worst economic crises in its history.

As explained in chapter 3, there were many contributing factors to the 2001 crisis, the culmination of a lengthy recession and a decade of neoliberal policies that caused rampant unemployment and destroyed the domestic consumer market (Vilas 2004, 574). In addition to reducing labor rights and dollarizing the economy, these policies led to an astronomical public debt, a spike in foreign debt, and a steady rise "in income concentration" (Vilas 2004, 573; our translation). Between 2000 and 2001, extreme poverty grew by 25 percent, reaching 35.5 percent of the population (Vilas 2004, 574).

This crisis flared in December 2001, when President Fernando de la Rúa and the minister of the economy, Domingo Cavallo, announced a "freeze on bank accounts and individual savings," a measure that became known as the *corralito*, triggering social protests across the country (Vilas 2004, 576; our translation). "The impact was particularly severe in low- and middle-income groups and in the economy's informal sector, where transactions are cash-based. The paralysis was especially felt in small- and mid-sized shops and manufacturers. A swarm of small establishments, personal service providers, and microenterprises were left out, barred from operating in accordance with the new rules" (Vilas 2004, 576–77; our translation). The situation worsened in the following two years: in 2003, 57.5 percent of the population was poor (Vilas 2004).

By signing a labor contract, Ramiro also became part of the superintendents' union. During the crisis, the building faced serious economic difficulties. In this period, employers first let go of informal workers to avoid paying severance packages. Ramiro's labor contract and union affiliation saved him from losing his job and becoming part of the "new Argentine poverty" (Kessler and Di Virgilio 2008; our translation). In other words, he was relatively successful during a time when many working-class people became impoverished: the hyperinflation of 1989, the flexibilization of the 1990s, and the crisis that accompanied the end of the currency board in 2001–2.

From 2001 onward, things were difficult for several years. Although Ramiro kept his job and did not have to pay rent, there was not enough money, and his family was forced to go without many things (even food). His mother also fell seriously ill during this time and required economic support as well as care. These tensions and problems affected his family life, and around 2002, he and his partner separated. The children continued living with Ramiro until they got jobs of their own and moved out. At the time of the interview, his sons were ages thirty-two, thirty, and twenty-five, while his daughter was twenty-eight. The two older ones had learned a trade and worked together for several years at a mechanic's. The eldest then decided to try his luck in the NOA, his father's home region, and moved to Salta, where he works in sales. His youngest son was unemployed. The daughter was living with a man who worked at the state-owned railroad company; she was a homemaker and looked after their two young daughters. The older sons each had two children as well, giving Ramiro a total of six grandchildren.

At the beginning of 2020, Ramiro had just turned sixty-three, with three years left to work before retiring, although he had already worked far longer than the law requires before men can retire and receive a state pension. The problem was that his state pension contributions represented only part of his actual labor trajectory. Many underprivileged workers find themselves in the same situation, with labor trajectories characterized by informality, unhealthy work conditions, a lack of protection, and precarity (Busso 2006, 140). For these workers, accessing formal employment takes years—if they can access it at all.

Labor informality among the poor is a structural phenomenon common to several Latin American countries and responds to dynamics of workforce exploitation dating back to colonial times (Quijano 2000). As noted in chapter 3, informality has been part of the labor market since the beginning of the twentieth century (Busso 2006, 140), but it expanded greatly from the second half of the 1970s onward as part of the neoliberal reforms that led to national deindustrialization, doing away with a large market of formal jobs (Busso 2006, 139) while simultaneously sparking a boom in informality (Busso 2006, 141).[10] As Ramiro's story shows, racial markers ascribed to the popular sectors are fundamentally responsible for their informal positions "in the labor market structure and different forms of exploitation" (Lázaro-Castellanos and Jubany 2019, 25; our translation). These markers made a core contribution to excluding broad sectors from "the right to formal, well-paid employment with social protection and the conditions for retirement" (Lázaro-Castellanos and Jubany 2019, 25; our translation). The mathematical expression of all this in Ramiro's life is telling: on the day he retires, he will have worked for fifty-five years, with no formal recognition for twenty-five of those years—45 percent of his actual career. This informality represents a form of appropriating the worker's surplus value with brutal consequences on the body: it takes a physical, mental, and psychological toll that leads to a loss of health. Under such a regime, "the body that is systematically punished, consumed by work, impoverished, and exploited is the one that is racially marked" (Lázaro-Castellanos and Jubany 2019, 25; our translation). In recent years, Ramiro has undergone two operations for serious health issues and lost a lot of weight. For a time, it was not certain whether he would survive. In both cases, he received good medical service, as he has a contract, contributes to his union's *obra social* (health plan), and thus has coverage for his medical needs.[11] He mentioned having the impression that his body was exhausted and that he needed "peace and quiet." Tacitly, he associated his daily work in the building with a lack of that peace and quiet. Yet when we asked more about this, his response was contradictory. He was immensely thankful for his job: "Everything I have I owe to this building: the little house I bought in Villa Dominico that I built myself. I owe everything—everything—to the building."

This is how we found out that Ramiro has a "little house" in a working-class neighborhood of Villa Dominico in Avellaneda, one of the eleven municipalities in the southern part of Greater Buenos Aires. It took him years to purchase the lot and build the house. The home is modest, he explained, but he likes it very much: "I like San Telmo, but not as a place to live. My life circumstances led me to live here. Because this is where I work. But I would like to live in the country. . . . This neighborhood [San Telmo] is all hustle and bustle; people run instead of walk. They live their lives stressed out. And, well, I'm here because of my circumstances. But I would like to live someplace else."

Ramiro finds gardening relaxing, and he has planted orange trees and other fruit trees on his lot in Villa Dominico. The fact that the southern district of Greater Buenos Aires was the only place where Ramiro could afford to make his dream of having his own house come true and build it with his own hands, is indicative of a phenomenon that Magliano and Perissinotti have described as the "self-built periphery" (2020, 6; our translation). Magliano and Perissinotti are referring to the urban marginalization of international migrants from Paraguay, Bolivia, and Peru, though the logic easily applies to internal migrants like Ramiro as well. The "housing trajectories of these people are expressed not only in forms of spatial segregation but also in the existence of a 'subaltern urbanism' . . . that organizes and structures life and the day-to-day for a wide swath of the population" (Magliano and Perissinotti 2020, 6; our translation).

Ramiro purchased the land to be near his job. However, he can spend time in his little house only between Saturday at noon and Sunday night, his weekly time off, before returning to his work residence in the building. Thus, he, like the elites who spend their workweeks in the capital city, has a "weekend home."

There were times when things were different. In 2009, after overcoming the 2001 economic crisis and after his children had moved out, Ramiro finally got together the savings to purchase his lot and build his house. His idea was to have a place for weekends, but his plans were initially thwarted. When the locals realized that no one was at the house during the week, "They stole everything! I'd lay down a brick, and they'd steal it. I'd install a window, and they'd steal it. So my assistant [the janitor, Gina,] took my place [as superintendent], and I took her place. That way I had more time: I'd start at noon and leave at five."

When given the choice between holding onto his position as superintendent (with its higher salary) or being able to build his own home, Ramiro opted for the latter. Gina became the superintendent, and Ramiro cleaned the building, did repairs, and looked after the garden, commuting from Villa Dominico six days a week. The arrangement continued until December 2019, when Gina retired.

The *Grieta* and the New Crisis

Gina's retirement was the source of a major conflict between the apartment owners and the building workers. She had reached age sixty but wanted to continue working. She was caring for an alcoholic ex-husband with whom she had reunited in 2018 after a three-year separation. He had a chronic illness that required constant care but did not have the money to hire someone: Gina took on the caretaking while also working full time, and they lived in the superintendent's apartment. In her telling, her physical strength was exhausted in less than a year: her back ached from lifting her ex-husband to bathe and dress him. Gina also suffers from arthrosis in her knees, but she continued working because she could not afford to lose the apartment and live only on her pension.

The owners of the apartments and the building manager saw Gina's retirement as a way to cut back on expenses since, given their seniority, both Gina and Ramiro earned a good deal more than new, younger workers would make. Thus, Gina was forced into retirement after a series of tense meetings with the apartment owners during which she was accused of being a "union rabble-rouser" and wanting to "feed off the state" as well as of having secretly retired to "illegally collect her pension and her salary at the same time"; she was also called "selfish" for wanting to continue to work. When we discussed the situation before she retired in December 2019, she was sad and visibly affected. She had begun to suffer depression as a result of the mistreatment by residents: "They've forgotten everything I've done. Years of service. They would wake me up at all hours, out of my working hours. They'd ask me to do the most ridiculous things. I never complained, and I treated everyone respectfully. I did plenty of tasks that weren't in my job description. Now they walk right by me without even saying hello. I was always against the union people because I don't like troublemakers. But now I think . . . they're right. We have to defend ourselves against people like this."

Gina departed, then, with a renewed awareness that she would not be treated respectfully in the building where she had lived and worked for so many years: her labor conflict was an expression of the border between residents—who self-identified as middle-class—and the building workers, who hailed from popular sectors. The owners asked Ramiro to return as superintendent in January 2020, which meant moving back into the apartment that had been his home from 1995 to 2009. He feared that if he did not accept, he would be fired before he became eligible for his pension: "I didn't want to come here. They asked me to come, and I had to. I like my house. There's nothing wrong with it here, but I like my house, you know?" He convinced his sister to move into the house in Villa Dominico to protect it, and then he moved back to San Telmo.

According to Ramiro, being a superintendent is a hard and stressful job. First, the residents do not respect his knowledge or his criteria for handling issues in the building. Second, because he lives in the building, he is expected to "always be available," a form of worker abuse.

> I know a lot about plumbing. And they wanted me to do something [in the building] but it wasn't the right way to do it. And I told her [the president of the homeowners' association]. And she refused to listen, insisted she was right. But that wasn't the case. She doesn't even know what I do here! I do things here for free because I like to help. You may not believe this, but I love this building. I brought up my children here; this was my home. They may well be the owners, but they don't defend what's theirs. I defend them and work to ensure everything is all right. I don't care if I get paid. For example, I have no working hours. I get up at six in the morning, and at six-thirty, I'm working. I don't take a break at lunchtime. Whenever someone comes looking for me, I'm always available. I like helping people. Some people come in at two or three in the morning and need me to open for them because they don't have their keys. And I don't get mad: that's what I'm here for, to help. I know this building like the palm of my hand—better than the owners.

Ramiro's statements reveal how he both has assimilated his exploitation and invokes ethics of care regarding the building. In his narrative, his life's most important job—that is, the repair and upkeep of the building—is irrevocably connected to his own life's meaning. For Ramiro, his trajectory—his children, his own home—is emotionally articulated with his responsibility to looking after the building, its plants, and its people as well. This ethical dimension is particularly difficult for the owners and residents to understand. They interpret it from a logic of economic returns, as if his work depended exclusively on a rational equation of the efforts spent on labor activities versus the remuneration he receives. Ramiro states that the residents' inability to understand and believe in his work ethic makes the fruits of his labor invisible: they have no idea of what he does for the building and its people on a daily basis. He provides an essential service, but his work is doomed to invisibility.[12]

Gina's retirement and these accounts by Ramiro are representative of a conflict between the building's workers and their residents—both apartment owners and tenants—that began to accelerate in 2015 for two reasons: changes in the neighborhood and the country's descent into another economic crisis cycle.

As explained in chapter 4, San Telmo was recycled as a neighborhood for tourism from the 1990s onward, causing a spike in the cost of residential real estate, services, and even basic household staples sold at local shops (Girola, Yacovino, and Laborde 2011). Since 2010, the city government has sought to evict the residents of the old *conventillos* and thus to clear the neighborhood of all elements associated with social marginalization. According to Ramiro,

There were many robbers. People would have their bags snatched. But that stopped. . . . The *conventillos* were repurposed, and those people were driven out. Now San Telmo is aimed at people with money, not at the poor. Now a poor person could never rent here. Because how could they pay rent here when an apartment goes for 50,000 pesos? They shut down the *conventillos* and drove those people out: the good and the bad. They gave some of them a place in the province [social houses located outside of the city of Buenos Aires]. They did this for tourism. There are no more poor people here. There used to be *conventillos* with poor people. And now only people who can afford it are left here. Because everything was designed here for people who've got the wherewithal, you get me? For tourism and people who can pay. In the past, a couple could make plans and rent a place together. But now, they can't rent a place: it's far too expensive! Just imagine!

In other words, the San Telmo that welcomed Ramiro in the 1970s no longer exists. There are only a few *conventillos* and squatter residences left: the neighborhood was subject to gentrification—with a certain degree of violence, given that the poor inhabitants, some of whom were relocated to Greater Buenos Aires, were removed. The rising cost of living in the neighborhood was accompanied by an abrupt impoverishment brought on by a new cycle of neoliberal policies introduced between 2015 and 2019 by President Mauricio Macri. Retirees are a particularly vulnerable group in this context. As noted in chapter 4, the accounts given by San Telmo's inhabitants reveal a drastic reduction in people's housing conditions and a rise in food insecurity among older people.

A good number of the residents of the building where Ramiro works—the self-employed, professionals, and civil servants that went to live there in the 1970s—are now part of this group of retirees that found themselves in difficult circumstances during this new crisis. However, young professionals are also part of this group. Due to the precarity and flexibilization of labor and the resulting obstacles to accessing rights, these residents feel less valued and less able to earn what they need to survive:

Yeah, the people here in the building are also fighting to get by. They can't afford the condo fees, or they have to do without many things. There is a young woman in the building who is a journalist at [a major Argentine newspaper]. And the other day, I was talking to the architect who lives on the sixth floor. He owns five apartments: he rents out three of them, lives in one, and works in another. So he calls me, and we get along just fine. People don't like him too much, but I don't have any issues with him. And he calls me to go to the young woman's apartment. Because, well, there was a rat there, and the architect says, "Let's see how we can solve this." And she says, "Well, I want this taken care of right away because I'm paying 5,600 pesos [US$87][13] in building expenses, and I earn less than Ramiro." . . . And she was pushing me for an answer. And I've got nothing to do with this: I went because he asked me to. And the young woman says, "I earn less than he does, and I'm a journalist." I felt bad. Because I don't decide my salary: that's up to the union. That's why we're doing OK: because we have a good union. But I don't decide what I earn per month or anything of the sort. If they weren't paying me that, they'd have to pay someone else the same. It really upset me because it had nothing to do with the problem, and she put me in the middle of it. The other day, a lady came up to me and said, "There's too many of you here." There are three employees [the superintendent and two janitors], and she says, "There shouldn't be more than two." And I say, "But who decided there would be three of us? You held an assembly and decided. You signed. I had nothing to do with it." . . . People are upset because they're being careful with their money. Everybody is careful with their own money. . . . They want the work of three people but with one less person.

This episode complements some information Gina provided and allows for a more extensive interpretative framework of the conflict between the building workers and its owners and/or tenants. Ramiro attributes his ability to weather a crisis to a certain safety net because he is unionized. He understands that the union offers him—like any other worker employed as a superintendent or janitor—the guarantees of a stable wage and a lower loss in real wages attributed to inflation, unlike what occurs with salaries in other labor sectors where unions are not as strong (like journalism).

This has strained relations with some of the building's owners and tenants. Because they earn more than some residents, Ramiro and Gina are seen as "abusers" or "privileged," two expressions tied to their union affiliation. Yet this is not only a question of economic capital. The conversation with the journalist makes this clear: she demands recognition of her formal cultural capital (a university degree) that, in her mind, should assure her an economic position suited to her status, which she believes is superior to Ramiro's. Her frustration with the situation goes beyond economics; it lies in this perception that she lacks the social distinction she desires.

Ramiro says that he has no intention of questioning the journalist's prestige, nor is he trying to match her in terms of social distinction. He also notes that in economic terms, union affiliation—not necessarily the formal cultural capital one has accrued—makes the difference in terms of worker protection. In this scenario, the journalist's dissatisfaction generates no reflection on whether a union might be useful in protecting her job. The position she takes is quite the opposite. She expresses a sense of unease that she conveys to Ramiro as if he were personally responsible for her feelings of downward social and economic mobility and the lack of acknowledgment of her cultural capital as a legitimate mechanism of distinction. In this framework, she moves to belittle Ramiro, expecting him to kill the rats in her apartment, despite the fact that this task does not fall within the scope of his job.

The connections among the crisis, the loss of the journalist's economic position, and her blaming Ramiro for this situation brings up a series of imaginaries and stereotypes of the political divide, a *grieta*. This division has been feeding hate speech with highly strategic campaign uses, which, as noted in chapter 1, have been especially conspicuous since 2015. These elements are captured in what the residents said to Gina in the meeting in which they decided to force her into retirement: "Unionized workers want to feed off the state." Her forced retirement led Gina, who had previously been wary of the union despite being affiliated, to eventually conclude that the guild offered her only protection against residents who ultimately "only look after their own money," as Ramiro noted. This is indicative of a constructed border.

I think that in the last year, people—I think everyone was upset with the hike in condo fees. I don't know what they are earning, but no one is better off than they were before: they're worse off. Everything is so expensive, you know? That's why everyone is complaining that there are three of us and that I make too much. Do you think I make too much? The fact is that people have no idea of [what it is like] being here. After all, I am on call twenty-four hours [a day]. People have no idea. They think it's all so easy. And they never put themselves in my shoes, only in theirs. Here in the back, there's a garden as thick as a jungle. It's a lot of work! Sometimes, the day isn't long enough. But they think it's all easy. There are sixty apartments here. Let's say there are two people per apartment—120 people. I am resting, and my doorbell rings. I get up, and never with a scowl because that's my job.

But there are people who say things to us that make you want to snap back at them.

To understand this strained relationship between subjects who see themselves at the opposite ends of a dispute about otherness, certain historical and contextual information proves informative. In Latin America, Argentina is well known for the strength of its unions. However, during certain political periods, particularly the 1970s and the 1990s, efforts were aimed at undermining worker organizations (Lenguita 2011, 137). In the last decade of the twentieth century, neoliberal reforms were accompanied by antiunion policies supported by a highly moralistic media campaign. This series of attacks led to a breakdown in the trade union fabric that had constituted the principal vehicle for struggle and popular representation (Longo 2007). This antiunion policy was introduced in conjunction with "massive, selective dismissals . . . from companies, many of them affecting workers with a history of union activism or agitation" (Lenguita 2011, 139; our translation).[14]

Yet the winds would change direction after the turn of the twenty-first century. Between 2003 and 2008, all of the Southern Cone countries experienced strong economic growth and repositioned themselves in the global economy. Both phenomena can be attributed to the renewed value of primary goods exported to international markets (the commodities boom). This process was accompanied by a turn to the left in the region's administrations, with political positions in favor of capitalizing states and promoting the redistribution of earnings by developing the domestic labor and consumer market (Svampa 2013). As noted in chapter 3, this process in Argentina was also characterized by a strengthening of the unions as a consequence of an increase in real wages achieved by different unions and intensified labor conflict and collective bargaining (Lenguita 2011, 137). Thus, unions reemerged, led especially by the guilds associated with different branches of Peronism (Natalucci 2013). This restored the unions as a central element in the provision of different forms of social protection and political representation.

Like most doormen/women and superintendents in Buenos Aires, Ramiro and Gina are affiliated with the Sindicato Único de Trabajadores de Edificios de Renta y Horizontal (Rental Properties and Condominium Union, SUTERH), one of the most powerful Peronist trade unions in the country.[15] In the Peronist world of trade unions and politics, many groups with varying agendas come together.[16] The support and close ties between SUTERH and Presidents Néstor and Cristina Kirchner (2003–15) led the union to be associated with Kirchnerism, pigeonholing it within the Peronist framework to some degree.

Following its success at the polls in 2011, Kirchnerism wagered on polarization, "aiming for its own political force to become increasingly homogeneous" (Grimson 2019, 310; our translation). Its effects, however, were contradictory. For example, it drove the opposition to form a coalition that began insistently using polarized language, progressively reinstating the political use of hate speech with some degree of success. As a result, Kirchnerism was increasingly associated with unionism, the workers, and the popular sectors, terms that became synonymous with thieves, deviants, the uncivilized, and the immoral. This polarization reconstructs anti-Peronism's political uses, a familiar trope in Argentina, with new layers of complexity, recovering their "racist and misogynistic" overtones (Grimson 2019, 313; our translation).[17] This polarization and the building of this antipopular and anti-Kirchnerist hate speech are essential to understanding Macri's 2015 presidential victory and his subsequent administration (Grimson 2019).[18]

Neoliberal reforms and the deregulation of financial capital between 2015 and 2019 led to an exponential rise in public debt, plunging Argentina into a recession that explains the impoverishment not only of the retirees living in the building but also of professionals like the young journalist. Once in power, Macri and his supporters exacerbated this political polarization. "One of the main rules of Macri's government was to appear as the opposite of Kirchnerism. The more below par the workings of the economy under Macri, the more his administration attacked Kirchnerism and spoke of 'inheriting a burden,' describing Argentina as a broken, 'looted' country. Polarizing the political divide to an extreme and greater depth was the only way to respond to [the Macri administration's] recurring failures" (Grimson 2019, 314; our translation).

At the end of his term in 2019, the rapid deterioration of living conditions in Argentina reduced the effectiveness of this type of discourse for a broad majority at the polls: 48.24 percent voted for the Frente de Todos [Front of All] presidential candidate, Alberto Fernández, who beat Macri and was sworn in with Cristina Kirchner as vice president. Yet 40.28 percent voted for Macri. For a good number of these voters, a symbolic association persists: workers, unions, and Peronism are still to blame for all the country's troubles. The conflicts Ramiro and Gina faced between the end of 2019 and the beginning of 2020 are indicative of the number of building residents who assign them a social identity at the other end of the spectrum: a frontier between the popular sectors and the middle classes. The middle classes see the popular sectors in a negative light—as unwanted others. Precisely because Ramiro feared the repercussions of this identification, he decided to accept the offer and become superintendent again; despite the pull of higher wages, he would have preferred not to return because of the emotional, relational, and health toll the job involves.

There are some nuances here. First, particularly for Ramiro, the association with this "negative" identity (unionist, Peronist, worker) overlaps racial labels connected with his origins in the country's interior. As Grimson (2019) notes, both anti-Peronism and anti-Kirchnerism are constructed along racial boundaries, and Ramiro embodies one of the marginalized extremes of this symbolic racialized construction of the social field. He is an internal migrant within Argentina's borders, a Black. The resurgence of expressions of hatred against the building workers pushes Ramiro to an "extremely passive" position: he must subtly navigate this process in which he is once again pigeonholed as Black, a condition that he both embraces and rejects.

Second, the assumption that Ramiro is privileged entails a complete lack of awareness of his life experiences during this crisis. Father of four and grandfather of six, he is the only worker in his family with a salary that covers living costs. The precarity of the work conditions and wages of his children, combined with the difficulties they faced trying to obtain employment that offered the same social protection Ramiro's job provides, forced him to become the breadwinner during hard times. Between 2015 and 2019, Ramiro used his salary to cover the needs of the family network.

I'm going to share my experience of this crisis. My children did [experience hardship], but I did not. Maybe it's because we have a very good union, and I've earned a good living. I've always earned—not sure if I'd say a lot, but enough to get by. But my children haven't. I've never gone hungry, but my children have. My children have, but I help them out. That's when they call me—when they don't have anything to eat, you see? [Last month] I made 50,000 pesos [his salary; $US780]. That's enough for me but not enough to save because I have six grandchildren. There are hundreds of buildings here in Buenos Aires. They all have building superintendents. So in that regard, we're more or less fine. We're not doing so bad, those of us who are part of the condo union. But my children earn 18,000 pesos [$US280] a month. And they're in a state-run company. Do you get me? . . . They work from eight to six. The one who earns the most makes 22,000 [pesos per month; $US343] for working a full day. The youngest earns 18,000 or 19,000. That's why I'm telling you; we're doing fine, we have a strong union.

Third, his social position is far from privileged in Argentina. When we asked Ramiro to rank himself on a scale of one to ten, where the poorest was a one and the richest was a ten, he explained that he was not among the privileged: "Compared to other people, I'm a millionaire. Compared to other people who work, the people who'd be a one or a two. Do you get me? That's my way of seeing things. I'd be a four, if I had to guess. I know I'm much better off than some. . . . I don't know how to rank myself in terms of social class. I just want everything to go well and for people to have something to eat. I am working class."

Ramiro did not understand why the building residents did not reserve their irritation for the truly rich instead of directing it at him. He wasn't the poorest, that was true, but he was far from being the richest. At the end of his explanation, he also reveals another fundamental element: beyond the number he assigns himself in terms of his income, Ramiro associates his social class with values. He did not know exactly where to put himself on a numeric scale because what defined him was the (moral) desire for "everything to go well" and "for people to have something to eat." Ramiro thus conveys that this value defines his self-assigned class.

In March 2020, two months after returning to his job as superintendent and a few days before the country imposed its COVID-19 lockdown, Ramiro suffered a stroke brought on by high blood pressure. He was alone in his apartment when it occurred. After being rushed to the emergency room, he spent several weeks in the hospital before returning to work. When we visited him after the incident, he said that the doctors attributed the stroke to the hassles and concerns he was bottling up. Blood pressure rises, he explained, when one does not express one's troubles. He believed that the increase in his blood pressure resulted from returning to his job as superintendent, having to endure it all without saying a word, being "extremely passive." He added that he was counting the days until he could retire and return to the NOA. He was planning to settle down in Salta, not Tucumán, because living is less expensive there, and he could enjoy the peace and quiet of the countryside. Throughout Argentina's March–November 2020 lockdown, Ramiro stayed in the building in San Telmo: he said he was "looking after" all the residents over age sixty-five who had been told to avoid leaving the house. He would go out to get their food and medicine, keep family members abreast of their situation, and knock on the doors of everyone who lived alone at least once a day to see how they were doing. Thus, the same residents who had accused the building workers at the end of 2019 of being "unionized abusers" had their basic needs covered thanks to Ramiro's care ethic, which, in his own telling, is what makes him a true member of the working class.

Chapter Six

Closing Remarks

Social Classes as Ethnographic Situations

Several anthropological reflections emerge from Ramiro's trajectory and its overlap with processes in San Telmo and Argentine history. This chapter focuses on five aspects that contribute to an ethnographically situated definition of social classes. These five aspects reveal different ways of articulating Ramiro's experience with race, class, and gender assignments.

Intersectionality

Ramiro's narrative clearly reveals how both external definitions of his identity assignments and his own definitions are situation-bound and change as a result of migration flows and social disruptions. Over the course of his trajectory, Ramiro has been Indian, Black, and Morocho. He was poor, an informal worker, and then a union member and formal worker. Though he has always been seen as a man, his masculinity has been challenged by external masculinities. One example of this is the police, who can repress him at their will, as they did with the young men without IDs. Thus, his trajectory indicates how social positions come together at the intersection of asymmetrical social classifications, rife with inequalities.

Thus, our first theoretical and analytical focus is on the perception of class as a construction mainly articulated by racial and patriarchal hierarchies (Kalb 2015b, 14). This means assuming that class perception is intrinsically intersectional, crisscrossed by a set of inequality markers that shape the social experiences of groups of people. As we saw in chapter 2, Black feminism developed the concept of intersectionality in the 1990s. As initially formulated, it referred to the fact that women suffer the intersection of diverse elements that determine social exclusion and consequently experience an accumulation of social inequalities associated with their ethnicity, race, class, and age (Crenshaw 1991, 1244).

Through Ramiro's history, it is possible to infer how an anthropological understanding of class relations comes together. It requires an analysis of the set of racial, ethnicizing, and gender relations that subjects face and that simultaneously institutionalize types of behavior, notions of identity, social practices, performances, and narrative constructions central to the functioning of national communities. The interviewee's place of origin and his experience as a rural-urban migrant offer the first of several definitions regarding his positions in an intricate tangle of social classifications in current-day Argentina. Returning to Grimson, we have seen how a political imaginary took shape during the twentieth century in which class labels ("workers," *"descamisados," "pies descalzos"*) were combined with both racial (*"cabecitas negras"*) and political ones ("Peronists") (Grimson 2019, 61–65). In our view, this symbolic construction led to an intersectional structuring of the daily identity relations between classes.

Configuration

Second, Ramiro's story reveals that the feminist concept of intersectionality proves relevant for exploring the type of identity relations experienced in the trajectories of subjects who combine different grounds for social otherness. On the one hand, Ramiro teaches us that the impact of these determinants is situational and can change depending on the context. On the other hand, Ramiro also demonstrates how subjects find ways of adapting and maneuvering these elements as they position and situate themselves in their interactions. Thus, a situational and intersectional perspective on these determining factors of exclusion allows the subjects' possibilities for agency to emerge at the interstices and reveals the gradual, contextual, and historical aspects of the conflicts that make them who they are.

According to this perspective, class is "a generic name for this

bundle of unstable, uneven, contradictory and antagonistic relational interdependences, a 'configuration' in Norbert Elias's terms"
(Kalb 2015b, 14). This means assuming class as a contextual phenomenon, one that exists within a concrete set of relations that
"does not refer to this group or that, to this position or that, to
this factor or that. Rather, it encapsulates a political and intellectual effort to point to the problematic of shifting, interconnected
and antagonistic social inequalities" (Kalb 2015b, 14). This concrete set of relations builds on local history and the articulations
among relational, national, and global historicity. The contextualization of class—its existence in a concrete social space like that
of San Telmo—implies observing its two dimensions. First, class
contextualization is a comprehensive set of expressions of global
(dis)equilibrium in a specific place. Second, a situational facet of
this contextualization is embodied in the people and their trajectories, involving a series of inequalities and the myths, ideologies,
and mythologies surrounding social production and reproduction
(Kalb 2015b, 14).

This specific context of existing class relations constitutes a "cultural configuration," as referred to by Grimson (2011). This concept points to the existence of a concrete social space, a "framework of complex articulations of social heterogeneity that is shared
by actors in conflict or different from one another" (Grimson 2011,
172; our translation). It also encompasses the fields of possibility
of this shared framework: the practices, representations, or institutions that effectively exist or are possible (be they hegemonic or
counterhegemonic). Though quite diverse, cultural configuration
yields a sort of totality when a certain level of relations exists among
its components. Thus, the individuals and their social sectors have
a shared symbolic plot that can include contradictory meanings
(Grimson 2011, 172–74). In this configuration, subjects have certain
room for action in the face of structural conditions, thereby suggest-
ing a theory of conflict, assuming that the local context is built from
confrontation (between class legitimation and transformation).

Friction

A situational and contextualized experience of class means defining it as conflict. In this regard, extrapolating from the theory of identities put forth by Cardoso de Oliveira (1963), we propose that classes can be approached from a framework similar to the one he uses to define ethnic groups and their boundaries. In this regard, classes cannot be considered totalities in and of themselves; they would instead be configured through the process of interaction— the conflict—with other classes. For this reason, an anthropological approach to the phenomenon should focus on the situation and the situational aspects of the parties who experience the conflict (Cardoso de Oliveira 1963, 34).

In concrete terms, the social situation is seen in this framework as the only locus where it is possible to observe the mediation between crystallized forms of experiencing identity—that is, subjective and group processes of identification on the one hand and the structural conflicts between groups on the other. Such conflicts interact to build the boundaries that define being or not being part of a community. Social classes can come together only when actors classify themselves and others through their positioning, situation, or identity for the purposes of interaction. Therefore, the only way to attain an ethnographic understanding of class is through the observation of the mechanisms that groups or people utilize at a specific historical moment and in a particular context—a "concrete situation" that organizes their "being for the other" (Cardoso de Oliveira 2007, 53).

This organization necessarily engenders a specific form of conflict that, to paraphrase Cardoso de Oliveira, we refer to as interclass frictions. We conceive of these frictions as "a form of describing the contact between groups that are irreversibly connected despite the contradictions—expressed through the (manifest) conflicts or (latent) tensions—between them" (Cardoso de Oliveira 2007, 56; our translation).

Diverse elements of Ramiro's testimony allow us to theorize how social diversity was expressed as friction in San Telmo. First, we saw how multiple social sectors gradually came to inhabit the neighborhood. This diversity left its mark on at least four dimensions of the neighborhood, as made patently clear in Ramiro's narrative.

1. The neighborhood "incorporated" a logic of constantly transforming its functionalities to fit the needs and possibilities of its new residents by creatively adapting the buildings that had been designed for an entirely different lifestyle, that of the aristocratic elites. This capacity for functional adaptation is a sort of identity marker in the neighborhood even today and can be seen in the way those new neighborhood residents have transformed its buildings and facilities (both private and public) over recent decades.

2. The neighborhood's spaces adapted to the necessary coexistence of different life logics and daily practices: the restaurant where workers ate was also where robbers divvied up their loot, and sex workers stopped for breakfast. Thus, while some families had lunches, thieves meted out their respective shares, drug dealers made sales, and prostitutes planned hookups, all at the same time. In short, the neighborhood's creative adaptability, its overcrowding, and the heterogeneity of its peoples and their practices made San Telmo's spaces polyfunctional. This is a spatial expression of a relational logic as well as the condition for the existence and reproduction of encounters between groups with diverse social experiences and identifications.

3. The experience of these spaces means that subjects must develop the flexibility to interact with social heterogeneity: they must learn to dialogue with others, adopting a strategic position in communications and contemplating the particulars of the languages and interpretative frameworks of different groups and subjects.

4. This logic of adaptive coexistence in the face of social heterogeneity in community spaces coincided with housing segregation practices. In other words, coexistence and segregation were also dynamics that unfolded simultaneously. Social and racial stereotypes were (and continue to be) employed as dialogue markers between the neighborhood's different groups. Therefore, we have seen that a polyfunctional logic of coexistence between diverse subjects and groups does not prevent racial friction from materializing. In other words, the racist markers structure the borders and boundaries of

interaction and the hierarchical positions of subjects, in both residential areas (with their segregated logic) and public spaces.

Contradictory Agency

The situational aspect of the experience of class takes us back to the question about the possibilities and limitations of subjects and groups in transforming their surroundings and the economic or political structures that comprise and/or penetrate them. In this regard, it is important to consider the action of subjects as part of a historical process—that is, as a series of continuities and ruptures that point to how they and their groups change their situational assignments over time.

Two contradictory forms of agency emerge in Ramiro's descriptions about adapting to the San Telmo building job. On the one hand, he adopted a strategically passive attitude with his employers. On the other, he symbolically inverted the identity terms *Black* and *Morocho* as part of his self-perceived identity. We refer to these strategies as contradictory agencies because they are situated halfway between reproducing and breaking away from these situations of othering; the tensions between accommodating and breaking away that yield these strategies. As Brito (2001) explains, through servile gratitude, the othered subject invokes the dominant subject's duty to offer a reciprocal response. In addition to reproducing the servility, this connection provides tools for interstitial action, thus engendering a contradictory relational pattern between identities connected by conflict (the Hegelian dialect of the master-slave) (Brito 2001). Scott (1990) understands that this type of uses of passivity configures the hidden transcripts of resistance.

The reformulation among subaltern subjects of the pejorative terms used by dominant subjects is a fundamental part of this process, serving as "compensatory inversions" (Brito 2001). These inversions, which are symbolic and identity-related, can recur in community relations, articulating popular social rituals with a great power to mobilize (Da Matta 1997). In Argentina, the articulation between servile gratitude and compensatory inversion drives a range of popular expressions. It can be seen in several of the identity, narrative, and performative uses among diehard soccer fans (Alabarces 2003), and it comes to the fore in popular political uses. This type of symbolic-ritual action has a strong element of resisting reality and implies a particular type of protest against the established order, but it also has the dialectical effect of reproducing the existing hierarchal system (Gluckman 1991 [1956], 109).

Ethics of Care

For Ramiro, class is an ethical resource in which he situates a particular morality, clarifying that his position as a "worker" involves a moral desire for "everything to go well." In his daily practice, this logic is indicative of the overlap between experiences that the social sciences of the past, in a highly bipolar reductionism, assigned to either the public or the private sphere. Ramiro took care of his family while he took care of the building, and these two caregiving tasks intersect, mix, and inform one another. He cannot dissociate one from the other. His class position therefore cannot be separated from the emotional ties that caregiving builds among worlds, spheres, and classes.

This type of work and the ethics he expresses have been historically attributed to women. Yet it is impossible to understand Ramiro's notion of working class, along with his masculinity as a working-class man, without considering his role as the caretaker of the physical infrastructure and people in a building that he knows "like the palm of his hand." His body, family, and ethics merge in an activity—caregiving—that he uses to distinguish himself from those who "only think about money." The union also appears as a characteristic that differentiates those who demonstrate this ethic from those who do not: the union cares for superintendents, protecting their salaries and defending their rights against those who do not demonstrate ethics of care in their work or their relations with co-workers (Lazar 2019, 183–216). In this regard, the gender perspective allows the meanings of class recognition to be extended toward factors generally not associated with masculinity. This suggests that certain social groups in Argentina must acknowledge the power of care when viewing their class belonging (Kunin 2019).

Notes

1. According to Kalb (2015a, 52), "the 'primitivist reflex' sums up anthropology's recurrent search for the 'pristine,' for the untainted, for the signs of ongoing non-capitalist aspiration or belief even in late modern times. As I will point out, this is one of the sources for the self-limiting anthropology that I am arguing against."

2. Measure based on multidimensional aspects such as consumption, income, access to services, education, and living spaces, among others.

3. Hence the importance of the form of capital that Bourdieu calls "social," which refers to "the aggregate of the actual or potential resources which are linked to possession of a durable network of more or less institutionalized relationships of mutual acquaintance or recognition" (qtd. in Portes 2000, 45).

4. Cultural capital corresponds to the knowledge and resources incorporated by the subjects and disseminated through their social networks. According to Bourdieu (2011, 214), three states of cultural capital can be distinguished: (1) incorporated, (2) objectified, and (3) institutionalized. The first is linked to the notion of habitus, being related to the body ascription. In the context of our study, this is a state that involves historical notions of otherness regarding the phenotype, formal education, aesthetics and presentation of people, and their way of moving, behaving, and relating to other subjects in public and private spaces.

CHAPTER THREE

1. The classic social sciences in Argentina (inspired by Germani's debates) conceptualized social mobility as *structural* (referring to access to higher-level positions) or *circular* (with the rotation of positions in the socio-occupational structure) (Dalle 2016). Social scientists also contemplated three directionalities of movement: (1) *ascending*, toward higher classes; (2) *descending*, toward lower classes; and (3) *immobility*, with permanence in the class of origin. The current century complicated these approaches by introducing the concept of *absolute mobility* (alluding to the amount and frequency of displacement between different positions) and *relative mobility* (referring to "social fluidity" and individuals' opportunities to move toward "different positions, regardless of what happens in the structural plane" (Jacquet and Clemenceau 2013, 4; our translation).

2. The work of Panettieri (1982 [1968]) was a watershed, approaching the popular sectors from outside the institutional framework structures. His position, known as "pessimistic," regarding the situation of workers in Argentina before and after 1910 analyzed living standards and housing conditions. His ideas were debated by Cortés-Conde (1967), who held an "optimistic" view of the effects of modernization for the poorest sectors. Leandro Gutiérrez's (1982) contributions worked on both perspectives, pointing out the limits of the sources used in the works that give rise to them.

3. Greater Buenos Aires is the area surrounding the capital city and comprises three macroregions (north, west, and south) each with its own socioeconomic stratification (Poy and Salvia 2019, 36).

4. The term *Revolución Liberadora* alludes to the dictatorship that ruled Argentina after the deposition of the elected president, Juan Domingo Perón, closing Congress, the Supreme Court of Justice and the rest of the judicial system, and removing the authority of provincial, municipal, and university leaders.

5. The renunciation of the relevance of the working-class identity was not total, as exemplified by the writings of Lobato and Suriano (1993), who initiated a theoretical-methodological reflection on different problems associated with and connected to the experience of workers and popular sectors.

6. The 2008 agricultural strike was a conflict led by agribusiness organizations in opposition to President Cristina Fernández de Kirchner's Resolution 125/2008, establishing a change in state taxes on grain exports (soybean, wheat, and corn).

7. In the 2007 presidential election, there was talk, as in the 1960s, of the *"gorillismo* [gorilism, anti-Peronism] of the middle class" as a consequence of certain interpretations of the electoral result that sought to crystallize the distinction between a popular vote supporting Kirchnerism and another supposedly free, autonomous, and more legitimate one from the middle classes to the opposition candidate, the UCR's Elisa Carrió (Adamovsky 2009b, 485).

CHAPTER FOUR

1. In ECM, conflictive interactions are referred to as "social situations," and thus the method is also known as situational analysis. Social situations are defined as a series of specific incidents "affecting the same persons or groups, through a long period of time, and showing how these incidents, these cases, are related to the development and change of social relations" (Gluckman 2006 [1961], 17).

2. In keeping with ethical research protocols, we assured that the surveys and qualitative interviews were anonymous and asked participants to choose pseudonyms or use their initials to protect their identities.

3. In the 2010 census, the neighborhood population stood at 20,453 (9,639 men and 10,814 women) (Centro de Investigación y Desarrollo del Turismo 2019, 3). More recent information on the neighborhood's population is not available. Official census information applies to all of District 1 and cannot be broken down by neighborhood, and the 2020 census was postponed due to the COVID-19 pandemic.

4. The subjects were presented with the following options: (1) shantytown/ slum; (2) neighborhood with housing projects/public housing; (3) neighborhood with an urban layout, sidewalks, and sewers; (4) gated community; (5) other (what?).

5. Scholars from the Chicago School of sociology developed the concept of "urban zones of transition" at the beginning of the twentieth century (Martínez-Veiga 1999, 13–14). It refers to areas where property values have dropped as a consequence of the dilapidated conditions of real estate, which in turn results from residents' loss of economic power and scant state investment in infrastructure. Properties in these zones comprise an infrahousing market occupied by the poor and by both internal and foreign migrants. Owners see an opportunity to profit without the need to make any investment, subdividing properties into more housing units and thereby leading to overcrowding.

CHAPTER FIVE

1. NOA includes the provinces of Jujuy, Salta, Tucumán, Catamarca, La Rioja, and Santiago del Estero and borders Bolivia to the north and Chile to the west.

2. Relegating certain national territories to the periphery is part of building national, ethnic paradigms (Segato 1999). This concept alludes to the logics and interpretative frameworks that allow for identities within the nation to be differentiated through a particular application of racism that has allowed certain social groups to amass power since colonial times. In Argentina, national identity is constructed through the contextualized configuration of long-lasting racial asymmetries, both local and global, that, when arranged in hierarchical order, frame people's social, economic, and political limits and possibilities based on the internal identity ascribed to them (Segato 1999, 117).

3. Karasic (2000, 154; our translation) notes the constant tension of NOA's "inclusion-exclusion" in and from the nation-state, which is reproduced through "scant or erroneous" knowledge in the country about the region's communities and local contexts). In the discourses of the local communities, this exclusionary ignorance "is embodied in different subjects: at times 'the Nation' (i.e., the national government of the country, as opposed to 'the

province'); at others, 'Buenos Aires,' 'the (national) media,' or more generically, '*porteños.*' The news produced by national media outlets, for example, effectively reproduces a metropolitan perspective that treats life in the provinces outside the Pampa region—and the social sectors that inhabit these provinces—as exotic others" (Karasic 2000, 154; our translation).

4. The testimonies and conversations with Ramiro that we present here were conducted in Spanish. The English translation is by Wendy Gosselin.

5. In his study of the geographic distribution of Argentina's population, Germani (1955) noted that in 1947, 62 percent of Argentina's population lived in cities. In 2000, this number had risen to 89.9 percent (Da Cunha 2002, 22).

6. The term *enclave* refers to a territory that is progressively characterized by a single predominant economic activity, controlled by a political force, or by any differentiating factor (a practice, a custom, a discourse) (Portes and Jensen 1989). These are the necessarily the only elements that unfold in the territory, but people recognize them as distinctive. Enclaves are also characterized by (1) structuring a social notion of borders between those who live inside or outside, thus generating (2) a sense of a specific identity (be it ethnic, group-related, or national) and (3) a sense of belonging that filters social relations and practices. All of this yields a visible spatial marker as the materialities associated with the enclave's predominant identity take shape (Portes and Jensen 1989).

7. This sector would become the new enclave of the well-to-do classes, creating a north-south border within Buenos Aires, an imagined frontier between worlds and different class configurations. The north side of town thus became synonymous with the wealthy, aristocrats, businessmen, landowners, industrialists, and politicians, while the south side was reserved for the poor, workers, national migrants (stigmatized as *cabecitas negras*), and international ones (stigmatized as *negros de alma* [literally, "black souls," refers to those who are deemed Black regardless of their skin color]).

8. In particular, the Dr. Ricardo Balbín freeway, built on an overpass above San Telmo, drastically changed the neighborhood's architectural landscape.

9. The concept of structural violence alludes to conditions of inequality stemming from an institutionalized approach to unequal rights on the part of a society's political and economic organizations (Bourgois 2001). The state reproduces this form of violence when it refuses to meet certain needs or respond to social demands or when it uses the power of law enforcement to repress subaltern groups.

10. In the 1960s, 60 percent of Latin America's labor force was, on average, informal. At that time, Argentina was an exception, with only 40 percent of its workers holding informal employment. Between 1970 and 2000, the country's informality rate rose 20 percent, while other Latin American countries experienced an average increase of 2.1 percent (Busso 2006, 142).

11. In Argentina, *obras sociales* provide workers with preventative care and outpatient and emergency services (in cases of illness, accidents, disability, medical leave, and pregnancy). By law, all workers who have a formal contract must have an *obra social*, and the premiums are paid jointly by the employer and worker (workers' contributions are taken out of their monthly salary). The majority of the *obras sociales* are run by unions; each labor/profession has its own (Maceira 2006, 2).

12. As Grimson (2019, 90) argues, both invisibilization and hypervisibilization constitute identity games through which groups that dispute the hegemony of certain spaces establish mechanisms to rank otherness. They are, therefore, resources for the political construction of hierarchies of otherness.

13. According to the National Institute of Statistics and Censuses of the Argentine Republic (2020b, 6-7), in February 2020, a typical Argentine family of four needed 40,789 pesos per month (US$637) to stay above the poverty line. The journalist, who lived by herself, should have been making at least 10,197 pesos per month (US$159) to avoid poverty: the condo fees represented more than half that amount.

14. As part of the breakdown of unions, the spaces for representation were gradually filled by grassroots organizations—associations, neighborhood movements, cooperatives—located in or near family housing and led by women (Guizardi, Gonzálvez, and Stefoni 2018, 47). This transformation allowed women's empowerment but also led to an excessive burden on them; they were now also responsible for community well-being in a context in which "traditional" mechanisms of political representation of the popular sectors had been eliminated (Tabbush and Caminotti 2015).

15. The guild was founded in October 1942 as the Sindicato Único de Encargados y Ayudantes de Casas de Renta (Union of Rented House Superintendents and Helpers) under union leader Jesús Santa María. In 1945, it was one of the unions that supported Juan Domingo Perón and established direct ties with Eva Perón (SUTERH 2020). It changed to its current name in 1949. Since 2005, it has been headed by Víctor Santa María. In addition to its *obra social*, which has two hundred thousand affiliates, the union has theaters, cultural centers, centers for technical training and high school equivalency degrees, a university, and a network of hotels, soccer stadiums, summer picnic areas, and recreational spaces. The union is also the largest shareholder in one of Argentina's most important newspapers. San Telmo is one of the main locations of the SUTERH network of facilities and services.

16. The resulting heterogeneity is exceedingly difficult to understand. Cerrutti and Grimson (2004, 47; our translation), for example, have suggested that Peronism can be "much more than a mode of identification": it can be "a popular relational culture [that] serves as a magnet for other orga-

nizational processes that not only slip away from it but sometimes stand in opposition to it."

17. On the political uses of anti-Peronism, see Jaureche 1957. Jaureche's novel, whose title translates as *The Prophets of Hate*, was published during the ban on Peronism (1955–73), when political freedom was severely limited. The work develops a critical analysis of the role of Argentine intellectuals in constructing antipopular and antinationalist hate speech among the anti-Peronist elites.

18. This victory was also tied to economic events at the macroregional level. In South America, the economic advantage of the commodities boom began to wane in 2013, followed by economic instability and a cooldown that conservative political sectors leveraged to rally opposition to left-leaning governments (Kalb and Mollona 2018, 5).

References

Adamovsky, Ezequiel. 2008. "Esa incómoda presencia: La izquierda y la 'clase media' en la Argentina, 1891-1943." *Políticas de la Memoria* 8-9:239-48.

Adamovsky, Ezequiel. 2009a. "Acerca de la relación entre radicalismo y clase media (una vez más)." *Hispanic American Historical Review* 89 (2): 209-51.

Adamovsky, Ezequiel. 2009b. *Historia de la clase media argentina: Apogeo y decadencia de una ilusión, 1919-2003.* Buenos Aires: Planeta.

Adamovsky, Ezequiel. 2013. "Clase media: Reflexiones sobre los (malos) usos académicos de una categoría." *Nueva Sociedad* 247: 38-49.

Alabarces, Pablo. 2003. "Algunas explicaciones, algunas introducciones." In *Futbologías: Fútbol, identidades y violencia en América Latina,* edited by Pablo Alabarces, 11-20. Buenos Aires: CLACSO.

Altamirano, Carlos. 1997. "La pequeña burguesía, una clase en el purgatorio." *Prismas* 1:105-23.

Arnold, Jens, and João Jalles. 2014. *Dividing the Pie in Brazil: Income Distribution, Social Policies, and the New Middle Class.* Paris: OECD.

Aron, Raymond. 1981. "Max Weber y la política de poder." *Papers: Revista de Sociología* 15:33-53.

Auyero, Javier. 2001. *La política de los pobres: Las prácticas clientelistas del peronismo.* Buenos Aires: Manantial.

Beauvoir, Simone de. 2018 [1949]. *El segundo sexo.* Buenos Aires: Lumen.

Becker, Howard. 1998. *Tricks of the Trade: How to Think about Your Research while You're Doing It.* Chicago: University of Chicago Press.

Beltrán, Gastón. 2011. "Las paradojas de la acción empresaria: Las asociaciones del empresariado argentino y la persistencia de las reformas estructurales." In *Los años de Menem: La construcción del orden neoliberal,* edited by Alfredo Pucciarelli, 221-61. Buenos Aires: Siglo XXI.

Benza, Gabriela. 2016. "La estructura de clases argentina durante la década 2003-2013." In *La sociedad argentina hoy: Radiografía de una nueva estructura social,* edited by Gabriel Kessler, 111-39. Buenos Aires: Siglo XXI.

Benza, Gabriela, Rodolfo Iuliano, Sonia Álvarez Leguizamón, and Jerónimo Pinedo. 2016. "Las clases sociales en la investigación social de la Argentina (2003-2014)." In *Estudios sobre la estructura social en la argentina contemporánea*, edited by Sonia Álvarez Leguizamón, Ana Arias, and Leticia Muñiz Terra, 143–214. Buenos Aires: PISAC-CLACSO.

Bourdieu, Pierre. 1977. *La ilusión bibliográfica*. Madrid: Anagrama.

Bourdieu, Pierre. 2002a. "Condición de clase y posición de clase." *Revista Colombiana de Sociología* 7 (1): 121–41.

Bourdieu, Pierre. 2002b. *La distinción: Criterios y bases sociales del gusto*. Mexico City: Taurus.

Bourdieu, Pierre. 2011. *Las estrategias de la reproducción social*. Buenos Aires: Siglo XXI.

Bourgois, Philippe. 2001. "The Power of Violence in War and Peace: Post-Cold War Lessons from El Salvador." *Ethnography* 2 (1): 5–34.

Briones, Claudia, Ricardo Fava, and Ana Rosan. 2004. "Ni todos, ni alguien, ni uno: La politización de los indefinidos como clave para pensar la crisis argentina." In *La cultura de las crisis latinoamericanas*, compiled by Alejandro Grimson, 81–106. Buenos Aires: CLACSO.

Brito, Bajonas Teixeira. 2001. *Lógica do disparate*. Vitória: Edufes.

Burawoy, Michael. 1998. "The Extended Case Method." *Sociological Theory* 16 (1): 4–33.

Busso, Mariana. 2006. "El trabajo informal en Argentina: La novedad de un fenómeno histórico." In *Macroeconomía, mercado de trabajo y grupos vulnerables*, edited by Julio César Neffa and Pablo Pérez, 139–57. Buenos Aires: CEIL-PIETTE.

Cachón, Lorenzo. 1989. *¿Movilidad social o trayectorias de clase? Elementos para una crítica de la sociología de la movilidad social*. Madrid: Siglo XXI.

Caggiano, Sergio. 2007. "Madres en la frontera: Género, nación y los peligros de la reproducción." *Iconos: Revista de Ciencias Sociales* 27: 93–106.

Canelo, Paula. 2011. "'Son palabras de Perón': Continuidades y rupturas discursivas entre peronismo y menemismo." In *Los años de Menem: La construcción del orden neoliberal*, edited by Alfredo Pucciarelli, 71–111. Buenos Aires: Siglo XXI.

Carassai, Sebastián. 2013. *Los años setenta de la gente común. La naturalización de la violencia*. Buenos Aires: Siglo XXI.

Cardoso de Oliveira, Roberto. 1963. "Aculturación y fricción interétnica." *Revista América Latina* 6 (3): 33–46.

Cardoso de Oliveira, Roberto. 2007. *Etnicidad y estructura social*. Mexico City: CIESAS.

Carrier, James. 2015. "The Concept of Class." In *Anthropologies of Class. Power, Practice and Inequality*, edited by James Carrier and Don Kalb, 28–40. Cambridge: Cambridge University Press.

Carvajal, Fedora, and Helena Rovner. 2014. *Clases medias en Uruguay: Entre la consolidación y la vulnerabilidad*. Montevideo: PNUD.

Casimiro, Flávio Henrique Calheiros. 2018. "As classes dominantes e a nova direita no Brasil contemporâneo." In *O ódio como política: A reinvenção das direitas no Brasil*, edited by Eduardo Solana, 42–48. Rio de Janeiro: Boitempo.

Cattaruzza, Alejandro. 2019. *Historia de la Argentina, 1916–1955*. Buenos Aires: Siglo XXI.

Centro de Investigación y Desarrollo del Turismo. 2019. "Análisis turístico de la Comuna 1, Ciudad Autónoma de Buenos Aires." *Boletín CIDeTur* 29:1–9.

Cerrutti, Marcela, and Alejandro Grimson. 2004. "Buenos Aires, neoliberalismo y después: Cambios socioeconómicos y respuestas populares." *Cuadernos del IDES* 5:3–63.

Cortés-Conde, Roberto. 1967. *El Progreso argentino, 1880–1914*. Buenos Aires: Sudamericana.

Crenshaw, Kimberlé. 1991. "Mapping the Margins: Intersectionality, Identity Politics, and Violence against Women of Color." *Stanford Law Review* 6:1241–99.

Cunha, José Marcos Pinto da. 2002. *Urbanización, redistribución espacial de la población y transformaciones socioeconómicas en América Latina*. Santiago: ECLAC.

Dalle, Pablo. 2016. *Movilidad social desde las clases populares: Un estudio sociológico en el Área Metropolitana de Buenos Aires, 1960–2013*. Buenos Aires: Instituto de Investigaciones Gino Germani/UBA.

Da Matta, Roberto. 1997. *Carnavales, malandros y héroes: Hacia una sociología del dilema brasileño*. Mexico City: Fondo de Cultura Económica.

Díaz, José Manuel. 2015. "Una aproximación al concepto de discurso del odio." *Revista Derecho del Estado* 34:77–101.

Duek, Celia, and Graciela Inda. 2009. "¿Desembarazarse de Marx? Avatares del concepto de clases sociales." *Conflicto Social* 2 (1): 26–55.

Economic and Political Commission for Latin America [ECLAC]. 2006. *Migración internacional, derechos humanos y desarrollo en América Latina y el Caribe: Síntesis y conclusiones*. Santiago de Chile: ECLAC.

Economic and Political Commission for Latin America [ECLAC]. 2012. *Latinobarómetro: Opinión pública latinoamericana*. Santiago de Chile: ECLAC.

Economic and Political Commission for Latin America [ECLAC]. 2019. *Panorama social de América Latina*. Santiago de Chile: ECLAC.

Evens, Theodore. 2006. "Some Ontological Implications of Situational

Analysis." In *The Manchester School: Practice and Ethnographic Praxis in Anthropology*, edited by Theodore Evens and Don Handelman, 49–63. New York: Berghahn.

Evens, Theodore, and Don Handelman. 2006. "The Ethnographic Praxis of the Theory of Practice." In *The Manchester School: Practice and Ethnographic Praxis in Anthropology*, edited by Theodore Evens and Don Handelman, 1–12. New York: Berghahn.

Frankenberg, Ronald. 2006. "A Bridge over Troubled Waters; or What a Difference a Day Makes." In *The Manchester School: Practice and Ethnographic Praxis in Anthropology*, edited by Theodore Evens and Don Handelman, 202–22. New York: Berghahn.

Garaño, Santiago. 2016. "Soberanía, estado de excepción y seres matables en el teatro de operaciones del Operativo Independencia (Tucumán, Argentina, 1975–1977)." *Runa* 37 (2): 5–24.

García-Canclini, Néstor. 1984. "Gramsci con Bourdieu: Hegemonía, consumo y nuevas formas de organización popular." *Nueva sociedad* 71:69–78.

Garguín, Enrique. 2013. "La clase media en el discurso público." *Cuestiones de Sociología* 9:1–3.

Garriga, José. 2005. "Haciendo amigos a las piñas: Violencia y redes sociales de una hinchada de futbol." Master's thesis, Instituto de Altos Estudios Sociales, Buenos Aires.

Germani, Gino. 1955. *La estructura social de la Argentina: Análisis estadístico*. Buenos Aires: Raigal.

Germani, Gino. 2010 [1962]. "La inmigración masiva y su papel en la modernización del país." In *Gino Germani: La sociedad en cuestión: Antología comentada*, edited by Carolina Mera and Julián Rebón, 490–543. Buenos Aires: CLACSO.

Germani, Gino. [2010] 1963. "La movilidad social en Argentina." In *Gino Germani: La sociedad en cuestión: Antología comentada*, edited by Carolina Mera and Julián Rebón, 260–314. Buenos Aires: CLACSO.

Giarrizzo, Victoria. 2019. "Macri vs Cristina: El balance final." *Perfil*, September 14, 2019, https://www.perfil.com/noticias/columnistas/macri-vs-cristina-el-balance-final.phtml.

Girelli, Luciana. 2018. "Discursos contra Lula e o PT: Expressões do ódio no cenário político brasileiro no pré-impeachment de Dilma Rousseff." *Revista Idealogando* 2 (2): 27–47.

Girola, María Florencia, María Paula Yacovino, and Soledad Laborde. 2011. "Recentrando la centralidad: Procesos de recualificación urbana y espacio público en la ciudad de Buenos Aires desde una perspectiva etnográfica." *Cuaderno Urbano* 10 (10): 25–40.

Gluckman, Max. 1991 [1956]. *Custom and Conflict in Africa*. Cambridge: Blackwell.

Gluckman, Max. 2006 [1961]. "Ethnographic Data in British Social Anthropology." In *The Manchester School: Practice and Ethnographic Praxis in Anthropology*, edited by Theodore Evens and Don Handelman, 13–22. New York: Berghahn.

Goffman, Erving. 2006. *Frame analysis: Los marcos de la experiencia*. Barcelona: Siglo XXI.

González-Bombal, Inés, and Maristella Svampa. 2002. *Movilidad social ascendente y descendente en las clases medias argentinas: Un estudio comparativo*. Buenos Aires: SIEMPRO.

Gramsci, Antonio. 1981 [1975]. *Cuadernos de la cárcel (tomo 6): Cuaderno XXIII, 1934: Al margen de la historia: Historia de los grupos sociales subalternos*. Mexico City: Era.

Grimberg, Mabel. 2009. "Poder, políticas y vida cotidiana un estudio antropológico sobre protesta y resistencia social en el área metropolitana de Buenos Aires." *Revista de Sociología e Política* 17 (32): 83–94.

Grimson, Alejandro. 2011. *Los límites de la cultura: Crítica de las teorías de la identidad*. Buenos Aires: Siglo XXI.

Grimson, Alejandro. 2012. *Mitomanías argentinas: Cómo hablamos de nosotros mismos*. Buenos Aires: Siglo XXI.

Grimson, Alejandro. 2015. "Percepciones sociales de la desigualdad, la distribución y la redistribución de ingresos." *Lavboratorio* 26:197–224.

Grimson, Alejandro. 2016. "Desafíos para las antropologías desde el sur." *Intervenciones en Estudios Culturales* 3:139–53.

Grimson, Alejandro. 2019. *¿Qué es el peronismo?* Buenos Aires: Siglo XXI.

Guber, Rosana. 2001. *La etnografía: Método, campo y reflexividad*. Buenos Aires: Norma.

Guizardi, Menara, Gonzálvez, Herminia, and Stefoni, Carolina. 2018. De feminismos y movilidades. Debates críticos sobre migraciones y género en América Latina (1980–2018). *Revista Rumbos TS* (13)18: 27–66.

Gutiérrez, Alicia. 2005. *Las prácticas sociales: Una introducción a Pierre Bourdieu*. Córdoba: Ferreyra Editor.

Gutiérrez, Leandro. 1982. "Condiciones materiales de vida de los sectores populares en el Buenos Aires finisecular." In *De historia e historiadores: Homenaje a José Luis Romero*, edited by Sergio Bagú, 425–36. Mexico City: Siglo XXI.

Heredia, Mariana. 2011. "La hechura de la política económica: Los economistas, la convertibilidad y el modelo neoliberal." In *Los años de Menem: La construcción del orden neoliberal*, edited by Alfredo Pucciarelli, 179–220. Buenos Aires: Siglo XXI.

Jacquet, Mario, and Lautaro Clemenceau. 2013. *Movilidad social y autopercepción de clase en Argentina*. Buenos Aires: Facultad de Ciencias Sociales, Universidad de Buenos Aires. http://www.aacademica.org/000 -038/467.

Jaureche, Arturo. 1957. *Los profetas del odio*. Buenos Aires: A. Peña Lillo Editor.

Jelin, Elizabeth. 1993. "¿Cómo construir ciudadanía? Una visión desde abajo." *European Review of Latin American and Caribbean Studies* 55: 21–37.

Jelin, Elizabeth, Pablo Vila, and Alicia D'Amico. 1987. *Podría ser yo los sectores populares urbanos en imagen y palabra*. Buenos Aires: de la Flor.

Kalb, Don. 2015a. "Class, Labor, Social Reproduction: Towards a non Self Limiting Anthropology." *Suomen Antropologi* 40 (2): 50–55.

Kalb, Don. 2015b. "Introduction: Class and the New Anthropological Holism." In *Anthropologies of Class. Power, Practice and Inequality*, edited by James Carrier and Don Kalb, 1–27. Cambridge: Cambridge University Press.

Kalb, Don, and Massimiliano Mollona. 2018. "Introductory Thoughts on Anthropology and Urban Insurrection." In *Worldwide Mobilizations: Class Struggles and Urban Commoning*, edited by Don Kalb and Massimiliano Mollona, 1–29. Oxford: Berghahn.

Karasic, Gabriela. 1994. "Fronteras de sentido en el Noroeste: Identidades, poder y sociedad." In *Cultura e identidad en el noroeste argentino*, edited by Gabriela Karasic, 7–14. Buenos Aires: Centro Editor de América Latina.

Karasic, Gabriela. 2000. "Tras la genealogía del diablo: Discusiones sobre la nación y el estado en la frontera argentino-boliviana." In *Fronteras nacionales e identidades: La periferia como centro*, edited by Alejandro Grimson, 152–84. Buenos Aires: Ciccus.

Kessler, Gabriel. 2016. *La sociedad argentina hoy: Radiografía de una nueva estructura*. Buenos Aires: Siglo XXI.

Kessler, Gabriel, and María Mercedes Di Virgilio. 2008. "La nueva pobreza urbana: Dinámica global, regional y argentina en las últimas dos décadas." *Revista de la CEPAL* 95:31–50.

Kopper, Moisés. 2014. "La invención de la nueva clase media brasileña: De la antropología de los números a las políticas de movilidad social." In *Clases medias: Nuevos enfoques desde la sociología, la historia y la antropología*, edited by En Ezequiel Adamovsky, Sergio Visacovsky, and Patricia Vargas, 87–112. Buenos Aires: Ariel.

Kunin, Johana. 2019. "El poder del cuidado: Mujeres y agencia en la pampa sojera argentina." PhD diss., Instituto de Altos Estudios Sociales, Universidad Nacional de San Martín.

Latinobarómetro. 2018. *Informe Latinobarómetro 2018*. Santiago de Chile: Latinobarómetro.

Lazar, Sian. 2019. *Cómo se construye un sindicalista: Vida cotidiana, militancia y afectos en el mundo sindical*. Buenos Aires: Siglo XXI.

Lázaro-Castellanos, Rosa, and Olga Jubany. 2019. "Precariedad laboral, segregación racializada y movilidad temporal de mujeres." *Quaderns de l'Institut Català d'Antropologia* 35:23-40.

Lenguita, Paula. 2011. "Revitalización desde las bases del sindicalismo argentino." *Nueva Sociedad* 232:137-49.

Lins Ribeiro, Gustavo, and Arturo Escobar. 2009. "Introducción." In *Antropologías del mundo: Transformaciones disciplinarias dentro de sistemas de poder*, edited by Gustavo Lins Ribeiro and Arturo Escobar, 25-56. Mexico City: Envión.

Lobato, Mirtha, and Juan Suriano. 1993. "Trabajadores y movimiento obrero: Entre la crisis y la profesionalización del historiador." *Entrepasados* 4-5:41-64.

Longo, Roxana. 2007. "El protagonismo de las mujeres en los movimientos sociales." In *Hacia una pedagogía feminista: Géneros y participación popular*, edited by Claudia Korol, 129-50. Buenos Aires: Pañuelos en Rebeldía.

Lukács, George. 1970 [1923]. *Historia y consciencia de clase*. Havana: Instituto del Libro.

Maceira, Daniel. 2006. *Descentralización y equidad en el sistema de salud argentino*. Buenos Aires: La Colmena.

Magliano, María José, and María Victoria Perissinotti. 2020. "La periferia autoconstruida: Migraciones, informalidad y segregación urbana en Argentina." *EURE* 46 (138): 5-23.

Malfa, Cristina Beatriz. 2004. "Intervención en barrios patrimoniales: Plan de manejo del casco histórico de Buenos Aires, San Telmo-Monserrat y su entorno." *Urbano* 7 (10): 31-38.

Masson, Laura. 2004. *La política en femenino: Género y poder en la provincia de Buenos Aires*. Buenos Aires: Antropofagia.

Manzo, Enrique. 2010. "Las teorías sociológicas de Pierre Bourdieu y Norbert Elias: Los conceptos de campo social y habitus." *Estudios Sociológicos* 28 (83): 383-409.

Margulis, Mario. 1977. "Inmigración y desarrollo capitalista: La migración europea a la Argentina." *Demografía y Economía* 11 (3): 273-306.

Martínez-Veiga, Ubaldo. 1999. *Pobreza, segregación y exclusión espacial: La vivienda de los inmigrantes extranjeros en España*. Barcelona: Icaria.

Marx, Karl. 2008 [1867]. *El Capital: El proceso de producción del capital (Libro Primero)*. Buenos Aires: Siglo XXI.

Miguez, Daniel. 2006. "Estilos musicales y estamentos sociales: Cumbia, villa y transgresión en la periferia de Buenos Aires." In *Entre santos, cumbias y piquetes: Las culturas populares en la Argentina reciente*, edited by Daniel Míguez and Pablo Semán, 33–52. Buenos Aires: Biblos.

Miguez, Daniel, and Pablo Semán. 2006. "Diversidad y recurrencia en las culturas populares actuales." In *Entre santos, cumbias y piquetes: Las culturas populares en la Argentina reciente*, edited by Daniel Míguez and Pablo Semán, 20–37. Buenos Aires: Biblos.

Minujin, Alberto, and Gabriel Kessler. 1995. *La nueva pobreza en la Argentina*. Buenos Aires: Planeta.

Minujin, Alberto, and Néstor López. 1994. "Nueva pobreza y exclusión: El caso argentino." *Nueva Sociedad* 131:88–105.

Murmis, Miguel, and Juan Carlos Portantiero. 1971. *Estudios sobre los orígenes del peronismo*. Buenos Aires: Siglo XXI.

Natalucci, Ana. 2013. "Revitalización sindical y sindicalismo peronista: Encrucijadas entre el corporativismo y la política (Argentina, 2003–2012)." *Les Cahiers ALHIM* (26).

National Institute of Statistics and Censuses of the Argentine Republic. 2020a. "Incidencia de la pobreza y la indigencia en 31 aglomerados urbanos: Segundo semestre de 2019." *Condiciones de Vida* 4 (4): 3–17.

National Institute of Statistics and Censuses of the Argentine Republic. 2020b. "Valorización mensual de la canasta básica alimentaria y de la canasta básica total: Gran Buenos Aires." *Condiciones de Vida* 4 (3): 3–8.

Noel, Gabriel. 2006. "La mano invisible: Clientelismo y prácticas políticas en la era de las ONG." In *Entre santos, cumbias y piquetes: Las culturas populares en la Argentina reciente*, edited by Daniel Míguez and Pablo Semán, 165–76. Buenos Aires: Biblos.

Noel, Gabriel. 2020. *A la sombra de los bárbaros: Transformaciones sociales y procesos de delimitación moral en una ciudad de la Costa Atlántica bonaerense (Villa Gesell, 2007–2014)*. Buenos Aires: Teseo.

Obradovich, Gabriel. 2016. *La conversión de los fieles: La desvinculación electoral de las clases medias de la Unión Cívica Radical*. Buenos Aires: Teseo.

Observatory of Social Debt of the Argentine Catholic University. 2020. *La pobreza como privación más allá de los ingresos (2010–2019): Introducción de datos fundados en un enfoque de derechos*. Buenos Aires: Fundación Universidad Católica Argentina.

Oszlak, Oscar. 1991. *Merecer la ciudad: Los pobres y el derecho al espacio urbano.* Buenos Aires: Estudios CEDES.

Panettieri, José. 1982 [1968]. *Los trabajadores.* Buenos Aires: Centro Editor de América Latina.

Pateman, Carole. 1988. *The Sexual Contract.* Cambridge, MA: Polity Press.

Pla, Jésica. 2017. "Trayectorias de clase y percepciones temporales sobre la posición ocupada en la estructura social: Un abordaje mutildimensional de las clases sociales: Argentina 2003–2015." *Revista Internacional de Sociología* 75:1–16.

Portantiero, Juan Carlos. 1977. *Los usos de Gramsci.* Barcelona: Folio.

Portes, Alejandro. 2000. "Social Capital: Its Origin and Applications in Modern Sociology." In *Knowledge and Social Capital: Foundations and Applications,* edited by Eric Lesser, 43–57. Woburn, MA: Butterworth-Heinemann.

Portes, Alejandro, and Leif Jensen. 1989. "The Enclave and the Entrants: Patterns of Ethnic Enterprise in Miami before and after Mariel." *American Sociological Review* 54 (6): 929–49.

Poy, Santiago, and Agustín Salvia. 2019. *Estratificación social, movilidad intergeneracional y distribución de resultados de bienestar en la Argentina.* Buenos Aires: Educa.

Pucciarelli, Alfredo. 2011. "Menemismo: La construcción política del peronismo neoliberal." In *Los años de Menem: La construcción del orden neoliberal,* edited by Alfredo Pucciarelli, 143–76. Buenos Aires: Siglo XXI.

Quijano, Aníbal. 2000. "Colonialidad del poder, eurocentrismo y América Latina." In *La colonialidad del saber: Eurocentrismo y ciencias sociales: Perspectivas Latinoamericana,* edited by Edgar Lander, 777–832. Buenos Aires: CLACSO.

Quirós, Julieta. 2006. *Cruzando la Sarmiento: Una etnografía sobre piqueteros en la trama social del sur del Gran Buenos Aires.* Buenos Aires: Antropofagia.

Rivas, Ricardo. 2008. "Dos enfoques clásicos para el estudio de la estratificación social y de las clases sociales." *Espacio Abierto* 17 (3): 367–89.

Rodríguez, Martín, and Pablo Touzon. 2020. *La grieta desnuda. El macrismo y su época.* Buenos Aires: Capital Intelectual.

Roldán, Diego. 2008. "La formación de los sectores populares urbanos en la historiografía argentina: Una mirada sobre el núcleo." *Signos Históricos* 20:194–232.

Romero, Luis Alberto. 1994. *Los trabajadores de Buenos Aires: La experiencia del mercado, 1850–1880.* Buenos Aires: Sudamericana.

Scott, James. 1990. *Domination and the Arts of Resistance: Hidden Transcripts.* New Haven: Yale University Press.

Segato, Rita. 1999. "Identidades políticas/alteridades históricas: Una crítica a las certezas del pluralismo global." *Maguaré* 14:114-47.

Segato, Rita. 2010. *Las estructuras elementales de la violencia: Ensayos sobre género entre la antropología, psicionálisis y los derechos humanos.* Buenos Aires: Prometeo.

Semán, Pablo. 2006. *Bajo continuo: Exploraciones descentradas sobre cultura popular y masiva.* Buenos Aires: Gorla.

Semán, Pablo, and Cecilia Ferraudi-Curto. 2016. "Los sectores populares." In *La sociedad argentina hoy: Radiografía de una nueva estructura social,* edited by Gabriel Kessler, 141-162. Buenos Aires: Siglo XXI.

Semán, Pablo, and Silvina Merenson. 2007. "Percepción de la historia, sentimientos e implicación nacional en Argentina y Brasil." In *Política y cultura en Brasil y Argentina,* edited by Alejandro Grimson, 249-98. Buenos Aires: Edhasa.

Sindicato Único de Trabajadores de Edificios de Renta y Horizontal [SUTERH]. 2020. "Nuestra historia." Accessed July 16, 2020. https://suterh.org.ar/nuestra-historia/.

Spivak, Gayatri Chakravorty. 1988. "Can the Subaltern Speak?" In *Marxism and the Interpretation of Culture,* edited by Cary Nelson, 271-313. Basingstoke: Macmillan.

Svampa, Maristella. 2005. *La sociedad excluyente: Argentina bajo el signo del neoliberalismo.* Buenos Aires: Taurus.

Svampa, Maristella. 2013. "Consenso de los commodities y lenguajes de valoración en América Latina." *Nueva Sociedad* 244:30-46.

Tabbush, Constanza, and Mariana Caminotti. 2015. "Igualdad de género y movimientos sociales en la Argentina posneoliberal: La Organización Barrial Tupac Amaru." *Perfiles Latinoamericanos* 23 (46): 147-71.

Torrado, Susana. 2010. *El costo social del ajuste (Argentina, 1976-2002).* Buenos Aires: Edhasa.

Torre, Juan Carlos. 1989. "Interpretando una vez más los orígenes del peronismo." *Desarrollo Económico* (28) 112:525-48.

Torre, Juan Carlos. 2010. "Transformaciones de la sociedad argentina." In *Argentina 1910-2010: Balance del siglo,* edited by Roberto Russel, 167-225. Buenos Aires: Taurus.

Ursino, Sandra. 2012. "De los conventillos a las villas miserias y asentamientos: Un continuo en el paisaje urbano de la Argentina." *Question* 1 (34): 68-81.

Vilas, Carlos. 2004. "Gobernabilidad democrática y heterogeneidad social:

La crisis argentina de 2001." *Revista de la Sociedad Argentina de Análisis Político* 1 (3): 561–89.

Visacovsky, Sergio. 2008. "Estudios sobre 'clase media' en la antropología social: Una agenda para la Argentina." *Avá* 13:1–25.

Visacovsky, Sergio. 2014. "Inmigración, virtudes genealógicas y los relatos de origen de la clase media argentina." In *Clases medias: Nuevos enfoques desde la sociología, la historia y la antropología*, edited by Ezequiel Adamovsky, Sergio Visacovsky, and Patricia Vargas, 213–40. Buenos Aires: Ariel.

Vomaro, Gabriel, and Mariana Gené. 2017. "Argentina: El año de cambiemos." *Revista de Ciencia Política* 37 (2): 231–53.

Weber, Max. 1978 [1922]. "Classes, Status Groups and Parties." In *Max Weber: Selections in Translation*, edited by Walter Runciman, 43–56. Cambridge: Cambridge University Press.

Weber, Max. 2006. *Ensayos sobre metodología sociológica*. Buenos Aires: Amorrortu.

The Authors

MENARA GUIZARDI holds a bachelor's degree in social sciences (2004) and a postgraduate degree in human sciences and regional development (2005) from the Federal University of Espírito Santo (Brazil). She hold a master's degree in Latin American studies (2007) and a doctorate in social anthropology (2011) from the Autonomous University of Madrid (Spain). Between 2016 and 2018, she carried out her first postdoctoral project in social anthropology with a scholarship from the Doctoral College of the National University of San Martín (Buenos Aires, Argentina). Between 2018 and 2020, she carried out her second postdoctoral project with a grant from the National Council for Scientific and Technical Research of Argentina, where she is currently an adjunct researcher linked to the Institute of High Social Studies of the National University of San Martín (Argentina). She is also an associate researcher at the University of Tarapacá (Chile). E-mail: menaraguizardi@yahoo.com.br

SILVINA MERENSON holds a bachelor's degree in history from the National University of La Plata (Argentina), a master's degree in social anthropology from the Institute for Economic and Social Development and the National University of San Martín (Argentina), and a doctorate in social sciences from the Institute for Economic and Social Development and the National University of San Martín and the National University of General Sarmiento (Argentina). In her postdoctoral project, she was trained in transnational studies through the postgraduate program in social anthropology at the Autonomous Metropolitan University of Iztapalapa (Mexico). She is currently a researcher at the National Council for Scientific and Technological Research of Argentina and an associate professor at the Institute of High Social Studies of the National University of San Martín (Argentina). E-mail: smerenson@unsam.edu.ar.

CPSIA information can be obtained
at www.ICGtesting.com
Printed in the USA
LVHW032137150721
692809LV00003B/509